A Comparative Study of Banking in the West and in Islam

A Comparative Study of Banking in the West and in Islam

Cheikh Soumare

Copyright © 2015 by Cheikh Soumare.

Cover design by Polly McQuillen

Library of Congress Control Number: 2015910729
ISBN: Hardcover 978-1-5035-8356-6
Softcover 978-1-5035-8358-0
eBook 978-1-5035-8357-3

All rights reserved. No part of this book may be reproduced or transmitted in any form or by any means, electronic or mechanical, including photocopying, recording, or by any information storage and retrieval system, without permission in writing from the copyright owner.

Any people depicted in stock imagery provided by Thinkstock are models, and such images are being used for illustrative purposes only.
Certain stock imagery © Thinkstock.

Print information available on the last page.

Rev. date: 07/06/2015

To order additional copies of this book, contact:
Xlibris
1-888-795-4274
www.Xlibris.com
Orders@Xlibris.com
705025

CONTENTS

I. The Origins of Banks 1
II. Banking in Medieval Europe 3
III. European Banking in the Modern Era 11
IV. European Banking in the Twentieth Century 18
V. Banking in Medieval Islam 20
VI. The Mudaraba in the Medieval Period 27
VII. The *Mudaraba* in the Early Modern Period 45
VIII. Mudaraba in the Nineteenth and Twentieth Centuries 51
IX. Conclusion 57

Epilogue: Too Much of a Good Thing[85] 59

Notes 63

To my beloved parents Gorel Soumare and Binetou Sylla, my wife Teresa, my daughter Binetou, my son Gorel, my brothers (Fadel, Leopold, Youssou, Cherif) and my sisters (Seynabou, Khady, Fanta, Dada, and Nana).

This book could not have been written without invaluable support from many people.

I wish to express my gratitude and thanks to four significant persons that have given me considerable encouragement and strength throughout my adult life, without which none of my accomplishments would be possible. These important people are my loving father (Gorel Soumare), my sister (Khady), my brother and friend (Youssou), and my uncle (Lamine Samatey).

I also wish to express my gratitude and thanks to all those who gave words of encouragement and assistance as I gathered this information.

I

The Origins of Banks

The institution of banking has a very long history which can be traced back to the ancient Mesopotamia, Greece and Rome. From these earliest origins there developed in later centuries two schools of banking; Islamic and Western. In this course we will study these earliest origins as well as the later evolution. A comparison of these two schools of banking and a relative assessment of their merits and shortcomings will constitute one of the main themes of this study.

When we investigate the earliest origins of banking it becomes apparent that trade was the main economic activity which led to the invention of banking. Invention of the coinage was the first step in the expansion of world trade. Yet, expansion of trade also required the development of payment methods between the seller and the purchaser, as well as the development of the credit system. The essential factor here was the development of financial intermediaries. Here the loan is made to the intermediary, who is trusted by the prime lender in order that he should re-lend to those whom he trusts.

"When a business has become specialized in such financial intermediation, it is already, in the broadest sense, a bank."[1]

Earliest banks existed in ancient Mesopotamia, Greece and Rome. The term *bancus* was a Latin translation of the Greek word *trapeza* meaning a bench or table where a banker displayed his money and his records.[2] Our knowledge of this earliest period of banking is hazy—no archival evidence remains. Yet, available knowledge indicates that these ancient bankers were petty usurers or substantial lenders, deposit-and-transfer bankers and money changers. They also engaged in trade and extended credit, thus commerce and banking tended to overlap.[3]

II

Banking in Medieval Europe

1. Italian Banking[4]

Italian banking appears to have dominated the early medieval area. The earliest references to banking are found in the Genoese notarial records of the twelfth and thirteenth centuries. According to these sources, the term *bancherius* was basically reserved for the money changers. By the year 1200, the Genoese "bankers" appear to have extended their activities to forming partnerships, accepting time-and-demand deposits, extending credit to customers and even participating in international trade.

Of these activities, formation of partnerships known in Europe as *commenda* is particularly interesting for Islamic bankers, as it has been shown that the Europeans have learned this technique from the Muslims. Indeed, *commenda* was the European version of the Islamic *Mudaraba*.[5]

The time deposits, on the other hand, yielded a return to the depositor. Yet, due to the intervention of church, this return was not in the form of an interest payment. There are, of course, documents which show that in some cases, interest was clearly paid. But more often, the return was in the form of an unspecified share in the profits of the bank. It appears that this type of profit-sharing arrangement substituting the rate of interest was applied between the twelfth and fifteenth centuries. This profit-sharing system known in Italy as deposits *a discrezione* was recognized by the church as usurious and condemned in the fifteenth century. A solution to this problem was found by declaring that the depositors were paid interest only when the bank earned profits, thus introducing an element of uncertainty so as to avoid being considered usurious. The solution appears to have been effective for we know that the famous Medici Bank operated this way in the late fifteenth century.[6]

By the fifteenth century Italian banks had become so powerful that they began to have considerable effect on the supply of money. The bulk of the liabilities of these banks was in the form of deposits. For instance, the total liabilities of the bank of St. George in Genoa (1409) amounted to 54.300 gold florins. In Venice the total deposits of the four banks doing business in 1498 exceeded one million ducats. *In short, deposit banking was well established in Europe by the fifteenth century.*

Based upon the notarial document, the actual functioning of the Genoese banks in this period appear to have been as follows:

1. The customers possessed bank accounts which they could use for payments by transfer.
2. Credits in the form of overdraft permission was practiced.
3. There existed inter-bank arrangements which permitted payments by transfer even if the debtor and the creditor kept their bank accounts with different money changers. In other words, it was possible to transfer funds from the account of A, customer of bank X, to the account of B, customer of bank Y, by writings only, without the use of specie. Yet this transaction could be done only if both A and B were present in person at the bank. That is to say, checks were not yet used and transfers had to be made by the word of mouth.

The Genoese records indicate clearly that up to the year 1200 money changing was the nucleus of banking. Thus, professor Andre E. Sayous was wrong when he suggested that banking grew out of credit or money lending.[7] Instead, we now know that manual and foreign exchange was the origin of Western banking. The manual exchange was performed by local bankers, who were not involved in international transactions. The field of international transactions was dominated by the merchants. Thus, unlike the later time when all exchange dealers are called bankers, in the twelfth and thirteenth centuries those involved in international exchange business were still primarily merchants.

These merchants used *instrumentum ex causa cambi* to transfer money from one place to another. This document, for all practical purposes, was the prototype of the bill of exchange. What was involved here was basically an acknowledgment of the receipt by a debtor of a certain sum in Genoese currency and a promise of repayment of the equivalent in *another currency,* in *another place,* usually the fairs of Champagne.

That *instrumentum ex causa cambii* was also used to disguise usury is indicated by some contracts which provide that a loan, if unpaid at the fairs of Champagne, would become repayable in Genoa at a predetermined exchange rate. In other words, such contracts involved an exchange from Genoa to Champagne and a rechange from Champagne to Genoa. It was Cardinal Heuricus Hostiensis (d. 1271) who recognized the usurious nature of such transactions. This interference was justified, since exchange dealings of this kind lost whatever degree of uncertainty they had by the fact that the rate of rechange was fixed in advance. This negotiation could provide the banker with an assured gain—a true rate of interest. No goods or shipments were involved and no actual foreign currency. The borrower simply had the use of money for X number of months while the bills travelled abroad to the correspondents, and other bills returned.

At this point it may be proper to spend a few minutes on the importance of the fairs of Champagne for European trade as well as its role as the first major international money market in Europe. From the point of view of trade, the importance of these periodic fairs stems from the fact that here the merchants from France, Flanders, and England met their Italian colleagues. In other words, the products of the Mediterranean were exchanged in Champagne with the products of Northern Europe.

Where products are exchanged, it is inevitable that money would also be exchanged. Indeed, it has been established without any doubt that there existed in these fairs also a well-organized money market and that exchange rates already fluctuated in response to the law of supply and demand. Yet, Raymond De Roover has shown that money as such was not brought to this money market in Champagne. Instead, goods were brought and all the transactions were made by an ingenious system of book transfers thus reducing the role of specie to a minimum. These book transfers were made by Italian money changers.[8] In an age where money supply was limited by the available bullion supply, this invention of book transfers must have played a vital role in allowing the economy to expand.

The fairs of Champagne lost their importance as the Italian firms began to establish permanent agencies in Paris, London and in Brugge. Another factor that played a role in this development was the development of the Florentine cloth industry which substituting for the Northern product reduced the Italian demand for Flemish cloth. In response, the Flemish had to find new markets for their cloth, this time in the Baltic, which heralded the age of Hanseatic trade.

As a result of these developments, new centers of European banking by the year 1325 were; Bologna, Florence, Genoa and Venice in Italy; Paris, Montpellier, Avignon in France, Brugge in Flanders and London in England. "In Germany, the organization of trade was much more primitive than in Western Europe, and there can be no banking where there are no banks."[9]

We noted above that the Italian firms set up branches in other European countries. We may now ask just how these branches were organized. It seems at first, that is during the earlier part of the fourteenth century, the structure of organization was quite rigid. The branches abroad were not legally independent units and the branch managers were usually directly employed by the mother company. They were provided with a power of attorney and were paid a fixed salary regardless of profits. If they were particularly successful, sometimes, they received a bonus. If they were unsuccessful they could be fired or recalled. This rigid structure failed at the first crash.

The new type of organization adopted by Datini and later by the Medici was basically in the form of partnerships. Each branch abroad was a separate partnership with the mother firm in Italy, each had its own legal entity, its own capital, its own partners and its own books. Branches abroad, instead of being managed by factors (employees), were placed under the care of managing partners who received no regular salary, but shared in the profits of the branch. The senior partners retained their control by owning at least 50 percent of the capital in the subsidiary partnerships. Other restrictions imposed by the senior partners upon their junior colleagues were the following: Senior partners had the right to terminate the partnership at any time, the Junior partners were prohibited to leave their posts; they were obliged to ask for the permission of the center concerning important matters such as lending to the sovereigns. If the senior partners so wished, they could always call the Junior partner to Florence to report.

The basic characteristics of these medieval Italian bank partnerships can be summarized as follows: The firm was made up of a parent partnership located in Florence, which had a controlling interest in several subsidiary partnerships. This arrangement had the advantage that one branch could not be made legally responsible for the mistakes made by another. This organization also increased the responsibility of the branch manager since his remunerations depended on his ability to make profits. Granting substantial authority to the branch managers was also necessary in view of the slowness and difficulty of communications.

The exact reasons for the adoption of the above-described organization at the expense of the older, rigid and unitarian type had not yet been explained by European historians. It is quite possible that the bank partnerships described above were a mutation and adaptation of the Islamic *mudaraba* into the European environment. Indeed, certain characteristics of these partnerships can definitely be found in the *mudaraba*. In general these Italian partnerships appear to have been more centralized and restricted versions of the Islamic partnership. We will come back to this point after we complete our analysis of the *mudaraba*.

The influence of the church in Medieval Europe was strong enough to prevent banks from getting involved in the discount business. So, Medieval banking in Europe was limited to the purchase and the sale of bills at the current rates of exchange. The Church considered it usury to demand anything above the principal on a loan so the bankers turned to exchange.

2. Avoidance of the Prohibition of the Rate of Interest in the Christian West

It should be clear by now that like Islam, Christianity also had strictly prohibited usury. Christians believed that in death the usurer carries with him his purse full of damned money and the purse drags him toward the infernal depths of hell like a millstone. In the *Divina*

Commedia, Dante recognized the famous usurers of his time; the well-known Italian banking families of Catello Gianfigliazzi, the Ubriacchi and the Becchi who were all at the end of the seventh circle in the rain of fire, each with a purse hanging perpetually from his neck!

Yet, gradually the church argued that if the usurer repents before he dies, if his widow is a devoted person and tries to appease God to favor her husband's soul by fasts and prayers at his grave, his soul may then be partially saved and goes to the purgatory instead of hell. And if she continues this for seven years, then his soul may even go to heaven.

In short, Christianity relaxed the threat of eternal fire and the usurer was given the hope of saving his soul. This is considered as one of the factors in the evolution of usurious banking in the West. To quote Le Goff, "The birth of purgatory is also the dawn of banking."[10]

Another factor which facilitated the evolution of Western banking in the path that it took was the above-mentioned bill of exchange. The contribution of the bill of exchange was to provide a simple and effective loan contract that fully circumvented the ecclesiastical and civil bans on usury. It did so by cleverly concealing the rate of interest within the exchange rates on bills. Since the usury was defined as a fixed, predetermined and certain return on a loan, any uncertain return was considered to be legitimate profit, a reward for risk. The return on a bill of exchange was uncertain and therefore licit because the rate of exchange might rise or fall before the bill was drawn.

Yet, in practice the interest was being charged under the cloak of exchange. The return on a bill of exchange was thus interest, plus handling charges, plus a speculative gain or loss.

There were also other methods for concealing the usury, such as including the rate of interest in the amount of principal stated in the contract (and thus deduct interest in advance) or charging a penalty for "late" payment, prearranged.

But much more importantly than any of these, it was the rise of Protestantism in the sixteenth century which facilitated usury in Europe. During the reformation, many Protestant leaders declared that it was not complicity in sin to pay usury. Luther, Zwingli, Calvin all approved of a limited rate of interest of 5–8 percent and condemned only the excessively high rates such as 50–60 percent. Thus, we have here, during the sixteenth century, half of Christianity beginning to deal in usury, fully sanctioned by the Church. This situation could not possibly have failed to affect the rest of Christianity (Catholicism) in the same direction. Indeed, with the French Revolution, when the church lost its might, even these countries began to deal in usury unimpeded by the Church. But the "official approval of usurious banking by the Church" had to wait until 1950 when Pope Pius XII declared that bankers "earn their living honestly."[11]

3. Other Types of Money Dealers in Europe

Besides the merchant-bankers considered above, there were two other types of money dealers in Medieval Europe; the pawn brokers and the money changers. Jews dominated the business of pawning and in Florence this domination became absolute when the Christians were prohibited to enter into this occupation in 1437. Of course, pawn brokers were not bankers but in the period in question they did perform some of the functions of the banks.

Money changers, by far the more important group, operated on a fractional reserve principle. At the absence of the central banks these persons had to operate at a high reserve. For instance in Brugge 30 percent cash reserve appears to have been practiced. Yet even such a high ratio has failed to save many medieval banks. The high death rate of the medieval banks was mainly due to the fact that they allowed overdrafts and they invested some of their resources directly in business ventures.[12] The fact that these money changers operated on the factional reserve principle implies very clearly that they were also instrumental in the creation of money. That is to say, they were partly responsible for the inflation. Yet, more importantly, by channeling the deposits into investments, these money changers provided finance for economic growth.

It was first in Venice in about 1520 that the potential of banks in financing war expenditure was realized. Banks of the Rialto helped the Republic to finance a war by creating credit against government loans. Soon it proved necessary to suspend specie payments and ensuing inflation caused bank money to depreciate in terms of currency. The same method of war finance was used again in the seventeenth and eighteenth centuries, always with the same results; a prolonged suspension of specie payments accompanied by the depreciation of bank money.[13]

Checks or written orders began to be used in the fourteenth century. Historically, the check derives its origin from an oral order. The bill of exchange, on the other hand, has its roots in the exchange or *cambium* contract.

The fifteenth century witnessed the decline of money changers, particularly in the Low Countries, where they were forbidden to accept deposits and to make payments by transfer. This policy was prompted by repeated bank failures which shook the confidence of the public and invited the hostility of the public authorities. Their disappearance made life very difficult for the merchants wishing to settle their debts. This difficulty was the mother of another invention; the endorsement. The earliest endorsed bill known to us is dated August 6, 1519 with a statement on it, *"Pagate per me a . . ."* (meaning pay to me to . . .). By the 1630s endorsement had spread all over Western Europe. Endorsement, of course, greatly facilitated the circulation of commercial paper and the use of drafts and promissory notes as money substitutes. Bills having several endorsements on the back have been found by the hundreds in European archives.

III

European Banking in the Modern Era

1. Banking in the Netherlands

To be able to understand the functioning of the Dutch banking system a brief explanation of the structure of the Dutch economy may be necessary. First, it must be mentioned that Holland was not simply a trading nation. This country also possessed a highly developed agriculture as well as an internationally competitive textile industry. Yet, the most spectacular success of the Dutch was in trade. Indeed, the seventeenth-century international trade was dominated by the Dutch. Even the English and the French had to bow to the Dutch hegemony. This hegemony was particularly strong in the Baltic, Atlantic and the Indian Oceans. The famous *Oost Indische compagnie* commanded a volume of trade in Asian staples that was almost twice as large as its nearest rival, the English East India Company.

This small country constituted such an economic focus in Europe that silver and gold flowed into Amsterdam from all over America and Europe. This American and European silver was first minted into the so-called *negotie-penningen* (trade-coins) than was used to finance the trade in Asian staples.

Two currency systems co-existed in Holland; a domestic one with a flexible ratio-to-international currency using a coin containing less silver than the face value, which made it unattractive to export them, and an international one using a high-quality coin containing a standard amount of gold, or silver in it. Those *negotie-penningen* which contained silver were known as *leeuwendaalderes* or the so-called lion dollars (stamped with lion) and were used in the Middle East and in the Indian Ocean. Arabs called this coin the *grush-al kelb* for by the time the coin reached Arabia the lion looked more like a dog! The coin that contained gold, on the other hand, was known as *rijksdaalderes* and was used in Russia. Thus, in short, the Dutch currency was the dollar of the seventeenth century and it was a metallic commodity—money.

The powerful economic position of Holland was reflected in the Bank of Amsterdam established in 1609. A basic difference between this bank and most other European banks was the fact that whereas most European banks were small, highly localized banks, the Bank of Amsterdam became a great international institution.

The basic purpose of the bank was to facilitate deposit and exchange. It accepted deposits in any currency above a value of 300 florins. It also had a monopoly of exchange. Any bill of exchange change on Amsterdam had to be paid in at the bank, which guaranteed payment and was in turn guaranteed by the Municipality. The bank was not, however, a credit bank. In principle, deposits had to cover any transactions in which the party was concerned, and therefore no credit was given.

These measures helped foster the image and prestige of the bank. Indeed, in 1672, faced with the threat of French attack, the clients of Dutch banks were seized with panic and many banks put up the shutters. The Bank of Amsterdam, however, went on paying out and from then onward, confidence in its was complete.

From 1683 the bank altered its practices to a certain extent. It began to give advances to individuals at low rates of interest and receipts for bank deposits began to circulate and to be exchanged as money. This was the birth of bank notes in Holland.

The main role of the Bank of Amsterdam was the regulation and redistribution of stocks of precious metals used in international trade. In order to understand the true significance of this role we must note that precious metals came to Europe from America not in a constant stream but in irregular bursts. This irregularity was mainly caused by the interruption of Trans-Atlantic shipping during war time. The sudden increase in the supply of precious metals normally would have wreaked havoc with the prices. If European price structure during the seventeenth and eighteenth centuries maintained a relative degree of stability this is thanks to the following practice of the Dutch merchants: When the market was flooded with bullion, this excess was deposited at the Bank of Amsterdam at very low cost and was gradually spent for business transactions. Thus the Bank of Amsterdam acted like a dam checking the torrent and converting it into a regular supply of cash—giving life to industry and financing trade. The entire European economy benefited from this.

The Dutch hegemony in European banking remained undisputed until the Seven Years' War (1756–1763). After this, English supremacy emerged.

2. Banking in England

Just as in the case of Holland, the development and eventual hegemony of the English banking cannot be understood without taking into consideration the economic, maritime and international power of England. Indeed, if late seventeenth-century England laid the basis for what was to become the world monetary system (the gold standard and banknotes). This was made possible by the English economic might.

a) Establishment of the Bank of England

The Bank of England was established in 1694 with the aim of ending a monetary disorder.

This crisis had occurred as a result of the war with France when the king had asked the merchants of London for a loan of £ 1,200,000 sterling, and they set up an organization to raise it. This organization was the Bank of England.

The king spent the entire loan on pursuing the war and the merchants, who had confidence in the bank, lent him more rather than keeping it among themselves. As a result the circulation expanded rapidly by paper money of various types. This circulating currency was eventually stabilized relative to international currency, thus laying the ground for the gold standard.

b) Emergence of the Gold Standard

We have seen above that the Dutch, through their economic might, had attracted silver to the Netherlands throughout the seventeenth century. With the beginning of the eighteenth century, however, it was England which began to attract bullion from the rest of the world with one difference, this time it was gold not silver which was flowing to the northwest corner of Europe.

This transition from silver to gold occurred as a result of the following developments: First the 1696 monetary reform in England led to a slight over-valuation of gold vis a vis silver; second, due to the 1660–1680 recession, world prices fell and the purchasing power of gold in terms of commodities increased; third, at the end of the seventeenth century, gold was discovered in the Minas Gerais region of Brazil. This gold, as would be expected, flowed in large quantities to England.

The mechanism and the groundwork for this flow was laid in with the Methuen Treaty of 1703. Methuen Treaty institutionalized the triangle trade between England, Portugal and the Portuguese colonies (Brazil) in exchange for the tariff-free exports of Portuguese wine to England. In this commercial triangle, balance of trade was always in England's favor. This balance was paid in Brazilian gold.

Gradually, extra manpower was needed to expand the Brazilian gold mines and the problem was solved by kidnapping large numbers of West Africans to Brazil. Between 1715 and 1727, the number of African slaves shipped to Brazil fluctuated around 2200 and 2300 per annum.

The sweat of African slaves as well as the sufferings of the indigenous population of America and the European adventurers produced ever-increasing quantities of gold out of which the following amounts reached Portugal:

	Kilos[14]
1699	725
1701	1,785
1704	9,000
1720	25,000
1725	20,000

The first beneficiary of the sudden increase in gold production was, of course, Portugal. But just like Spain in the sixteenth and seventeenth centuries, the final result depended on whether or not she kept the possession of the metal, that is, on the balance of payments. Yet, it was explained above that Portugal suffered a continuous balance of payment deficit vis a vis England. Therefore, Brazilian-Portuguese gold eventually flowed into England. Moreover, since England obtained this gold in exchange for her industrial products, the stimulus provided to the English economy was greater than if England had possessed gold mines in her own territory and mined the gold directly herself.[15]

As a result of these developments, large quantities of gold entered into England with which English mints minted £14 million of gold coins between 1694 and 1727. This influx of gold enabled the English economy to absorb the various forms of paper money that were in circulation. As a result, the currency was stabilized and was backed by gold. From 1720 until 1798 (Napoleonic Wars), England enjoyed a monetary stability characterized by the import and minting of gold.

In this period, silver more or less fell into disuse and became simply a small coin currency and gold, for all practical purposes, became the only standard. A law of 22 June 1816 criticized *bimetalizm* and affirmed that only gold should be the standard measure of value and legal tender for payments. Payment in silver coin was restricted to £2. Thus, for all practical purposes, the gold standard had been established. From this date until the First World War the monetary system of Europe was dominated by bank notes and gold. The overall stability of the monetary system was maintained by the convertibility of bank notes into gold at any moment.

3. Banking in France

The first attempt to establish a central bank in France was made by a Scotsman, Law, who was invited by the French crown to reform the French financial system. The *Banque Generale* was established in 1716 only to fall four years later. No new attempt was made until 1776, when *Caisse d'Escomptes* was established. During the Revolution this bank had to suspend its activities and the definite establishment of a central bank in France had to wait until Napoleon. In 1800 the name of the *Caisse* was changed to the Bank of France. By 1806 the bank was closely linked to the state and the executive authority was given to a governor and two deputies appointed directly by the state. In 1809 the bank obtained the exclusive right of issuing notes in Paris.

The need for credit in the provinces, on the other hand, was met by opening departmental banks in the chief provincial centers with rights of issue limited to prescribed areas. These were compelled to keep a metallic reserve equal to a third of their circulation.

Development of joint-stock banks in France dates back to the 1850s. The best-known joint-stock bank of this period was the *Credit Mobilier*, which, instead of confining itself to bill-discounting, also floated companies, financed industrial undertakings and speculated in stocks and shares. At first it was dazzlingly successful and in 1855 it declared a dividend of 47 percent. Eventually, however, the capital was tied up in various undertakings and in 1867 the company, unable to realize its assets, failed ignominiously.

Since the Second World War a remarkable concentration has taken place among the French joint-stock banks, so that six great banks enjoy the monopoly of banking in France today. Some of these banks in their early days ventured into company promoting but the failures of *Credit Mobilier* and *Union Generale* have been so discouraging in France that French banks still prefer to keep a distance between themselves and industrial firms.

4. Banking in Germany

In contrast to French and British banking, German banks have boldly financed industrial undertakings, not only with short-time credit but with permanent capital. As such, these banks have played a conspicuous part in promoting the general industrial development of Germany. Syndicates of banks have built railways, constructed canals and launched industrial enterprises. Bankers sit on the boards of all important industrial companies, and industry is subordinated to finance in a way that is almost unknown in any other country.

This influence of bankers has been a powerful factor in promoting the cartel movements in Germany. Having a financial interest in a multiplicity of undertakings, they have not wished to see their proteges slaughter each other in wars of competition and they have exerted themselves to introduce peace amongst the combatants. This they have done by the formation of alliances and agreements for the fixing of prices and the division of markets amongst the chief competitors.

IV

European Banking in the Twentieth Century

A basic feature of banking in the twentieth century has been the definite establishment of central banks in almost every country in the world. The relations between these banks and the governments naturally differ from country to country, that is, central banks enjoy more autonomy in certain countries than do their counterparts in other countries.

As for the private banks, the general tenancy in the West has been for these banks to merge. Now, most Western European countries are dominated by five to ten major private banks. This is in sharp contrast to the U.S. where small banks manage to co-exist next to giants.

Another feature of twentieth-century banking has been the establishment of monetary institutions that specialize in intergovernmental lending of funds such as the World Bank, the I.M.F. and the O.E.C.D. One of the basic aims for their emergence has been to spread economic growth more evenly among all countries. Though it is rather too early to judge, their performance does not appear to be bright, for discrepancy between the developed and the developing world appears to be increasing instead of decreasing.

Finally, a most exciting event of the recent years has been the birth of OPEC and the rise of Arab capital. Initially Arab capital was invested in the West through the establishment of commercial banks in partnership with the Western countries. Thus, the hopes of the Third World, particularly of the Islamic world, for a massive injection of Islamic petro-dollars appeared to have been in vain. However, the most recent developments, that is, the establishment of Islamic Development Bank with a capital of two billion Islamic Dinars as well as the establishment of Islamic Banks are new developments that generate new hopes for the developing world.[16]

We have so far explained the origins of banking in the West as well as its development throughout the Middle Ages. Several questions come to the mind at this point; Did banking in Islam develop out of the same roots? In what ways did banking in the Islamic world differ from the Western? Did banks exist in the Islamic world at all? In what follows we will try to answer these questions.

V

Banking in Medieval Islam

It can be interesting to observe how a simple sentence sometimes triggers specialized research. Such a sentence, "There can be no banking where there are no banks" was written by Raymond De Roover.[17] Abraham Udovitch reacted to this sentence and the result was an excellent article published rather recently. In this article Udovitch summarizes his reaction to De Roover's as follows:

> This proposition may hold true for the development of banking in Medieval Europe, but it certainly does not describe the Medieval Islamic world, (where) we encounter bankers, and we encounter extensive and ramified banking activities <u>but we do not encounter banks.</u> That is, we cannot identify any autonomous or semiautonomous institutions whose primary concern was dealing in money as a specialized, if not exclusive, pursuit.[18]

Thus, the last question mentioned above: "Did banks exist in the Islamic world at all?" has already been answered. This negative answer holds true for the entire pre-modern period, for the banks entered into the Middle East as late as the nineteenth century.[19] If that is so, how did the Muslims organize such primary functions of the banks as deposits, credit, loans and bills of exchange without the banks? We will try to answer this question in what follows.

1. Prohibition of the *riba*

Perhaps a good point to start our analysis would be the prohibition of usury which was common to all monotheist religions. We have seen above that in Europe the prohibition of usury had affected the evolution of banking, yet in time, the church comprised with the practice by introducing the concept of purgatory. Other devices, such as concealing the interest in the bill of exchange, were also developed, thus clearing the way for usurious banking.

By contrast, in the Islamic world the jurists did not compromise and the ban on *riba* survived until the nineteenth century.[20] If so, to what extent was the uncompromising Islamic prohibition against usury observed in actual practice? Did it inhibit the conduct of economic life, did it restrain or in other ways affect the process of commercial exchange? And how did it affect credit operation, money exchange and other operations normally associated with banking?

Having observed that there was a flourishing commercial life in medieval Islam, Western scholars came to the conclusion that in practice the ban on usury was simply neglected. For these writers the strong and frequent prohibition of usury in Islamic legal writings was the indirect testimony to its equally frequent violation in practice.[21]

The truth, however, appears to have been much more complex than this simplistic view. Based upon the findings of latest research conducted in the famous Geniza archives of Cairo, Udovitch argues that the ban on usury was very much observed in daily business practice *and* notwithstanding this, medieval Islam succeeded in establishing a commercial empire. *In short, prohibition of usury was not an impediment to the growth of commerce and economic performance in general.*

Unimpeded growth of commerce and economy with the ban on usury fully in force was made possible by a variety of other commercial techniques which effectively fulfilled the basic functions of the interest. These techniques included a variety of partnership forms, the *mudaraba* and other related contracts, credit arrangements, transfer of debt, letters of credit, etc. All of these techniques were approved by the religious authorities. They also had the advantage that the merchants were perfectly acquainted with them since some of them had existed even before the birth of Islam.

"Most importantly, because these alternate forms of investment and credit were a socially more congenial and effective means of economic connection, they were preferred over loans."[22]

It is thanks to the Islamic invention of these alternative commercial techniques that the prohibition of usury had only a minimal effect on the commerce and economic development of Islam. The same prohibition, however, affected the development of financial practices and institutions substantially in the West and may have been even a major obstacle to the development of western exchange and commerce.[23]

Let us now start studying these Islamic commercial techniques which constituted effective alternatives to usury.

Islamic Commercial Techniques

a) Deposit

We have seen above that deposit banking was a major feature of the European banking. In this system, deposits were first attracted by promising a share in the profits of the bank *a discrezione* and later when this practice was condemned the depositors were paid interest secretly by the banks. The deposits that were accumulated on the other hand, were loaned at a higher premium to the third parties, usually merchants or princes. Charging interest on loans was also done secretly. The influence of the Catholic Church continued to be effective on these matters until the French Revolution. Charging interest on loans was officially recognized on October 12, 1789.

This type of deposit banking is completely foreign to the Islamic world of commerce. In Islam conception of deposit emphasized reliable safekeeping pure and simple. The uses to which the depository could put the deposits were severely restricted. This stands in sharp contrast with the Western practice whereby the depository was permitted to use the deposited money for a variety of commercial purposes. In return for this privilege the deposit was returned to its owner with a premium.

Limitation of deposits to pure safekeeping affected the subsequent development of banking in the Islamic world substantially. What proved to be a potent combination in the West, that is, the generation of capital by means of small deposits on the one hand and money lending and the provision of credit for investment on the other, did not develop in the Islamic economies.

Another feature of Western banking was financing the wars or loaning to the kings and princes. This proved to be a mixed blessing for the Western banks—huge fortunes were made this way as well as many bankruptcies had to be declared. In the Islamic world emergency finance to the state was provided by confiscations, extra taxation and, particularly, by tax farming.

Tax farming was vastly different from the Western-style loan. It was basically an advance cash payment to the government in return for the right to collect the taxes of a tax source for a fixed period. The relevance of all this for the history of banking is that the private funds provided to the public treasuries of the Medieval Islamic world were not generated by accumulating and risking the deposits of many people, but were basically in the form of private fortunes and were in the nature of a high-risk investment.[24]

At this point we may ask the following question; "If in Islam, deposits were not channelized into investment through the deposit banking, how were such investments financed? And if a person had cash, how did he obtain a return on his capital?"

These requirements, which would be felt strongly in any developing economy, were satisfied by alternative possibilities available. These possibilities were basically either in the form of partnerships or *mudaraba* associations. Yet, every one of these alternatives had one feature in common; they were almost always personal relationships. That is to say, unlike the impersonality of western associations as a result of which the depositors never knew the individuals they were financing, in Islamic associations each partner knew the other quite well. By implication, Islamic associations had to be very small in size, again, in sharp contrast to what eventually became giant impersonal Western banks. Thus small size and decentralized decision making characterized Islamic commercial associations.

b) Credit

Credit arrangements of various types have been observed in the Islamic world as early as the eighth century. By the eleventh century, according to the Geniza sources, the entire Indian Ocean trade as well as the Mediterranean one, were characterized by credit operations. This should be of no surprise to us, for credit arrangements in international trade alleviated the problem of transporting large quantities of specie across often dangerous routes and in combination with other contracts they served to share the risks. Hence, buying and selling on credit was an accepted and widespread commercial practice. Moreover, credit sales—deferred payments for goods bought and advance payments for future delivery—were not only considered fully legitimate but were viewed as indispensable to profitable trading. Sarakshi, the eleventh-century jurist, explained this view clearly,

> We hold that selling for credit is part of the practice of merchants and that it is the most conducive means of achievement of the investor's goal which is profit. In most cases, profit can only be achieved by selling for credit and not selling for cash.[25]

In Islamic commercial practice, the *hawala* and the *suftaja* were the basic instruments for dealing in credit. The *hawala* was the payment of debt through the transfer of a claim and the *suftaja* a letter of credit or bill of exchange. These two financial techniques were in use as early as the eighth century and both made possible the transfer of large sums of money over long distances without the use of any specie.

It was also possible to form a partnership purely on the basis of credit without supplying any cash or other forms of capital. This came about when people formed a partnership without any capital in order to buy goods on credit and then resell. This arrangement was appropriately called *sharikat al-mafalis,* the partnership of the penniless. In conformation of the informality of the Islamic associations mentioned above, this partnership was also called "partnership of good reputations." Those who enjoyed good reputation were known personally and credit was extended only to such individuals, without any collateral.

These two designations for the credit partnership, that is, "the partnership of the penniless" and "the partnership of those with status and good reputations," reflect two of the major aspects of Islamic credit arrangements. The first reflects a situation in which traders without sufficient resources seek financing; traders hiring the capital. And the second reflects a situation where capital-seeking profitable investment outlet is hiring the trades. We will see these principles come up frequently in the following lectures.

The basic economic function of these arrangements were perfectly well understood by medieval Islamic jurists. According to Kasani, "The purpose of commercial investment based on cash was in the increase of capital; the purpose of a credit partnership is both the increase and *the creation* of the capital itself, since credit is a means for augmenting or creating capital."[26]

Moving from theoretical level to the practice, Cairo Geniza documents reveal clearly that credit transactions were most frequently used in the eleventh–thirteenth centuries. This basically took the form of deferred payment for a fixed period, and the buyer had to pay a *premium* for deferring payment. Consequently, there were two prices; one for cash transaction and a slightly higher one for a credit transaction. This practice was sanctioned by the jurists and was not considered usurious.

c) Written Instruments of Credit

The *hawala*, or transfer of debt, functioned more or less in the manner described in the lawbooks, and is encountered frequently in the Geniza records as a substitute for cash payment.

The *suftaja* as mentioned above was the Islamic bill of exchange or a letter of credit. It differed from the Western bill of exchange in the following important aspect: Whereas the Western bill of exchange entailed the initial payment of one type of currency in return for the payment of *another* type of currency in a different location, consequently leading the way for a disguised usury as we have seen above, the *suftaja* involved repayment in exactly the same type of money. Thus the *suftaja* made it impossible to hide any usurious transactions and consequently the so-called "dry exchange" did not develop in the Islamic commerce.[27]

Suftajas were issued by and drawn upon well-known bankers, and a high fee was charged for their issue. They were as good as money and could be cashed only by the person to whom they were made out, and only in the place where they were assigned.

In addition to the *hawala* and *suftaja* there was the *rug'a* which designated a broad category of credit papers used for smaller payments in local trade. The *rug'a* was basically similar to the modern check.

All of these instruments of credit described above were totally overshadowed by a remarkable institution, the Islamic *mudaraba*. This vastly important institution which survived from pre-Islamic times to the twentieth century and was used extensively from the Arabian desert to Europe in the West and to Indonesia in the East will be discussed in the coming lectures.

VI

The Mudaraba in the Medieval Period

In the medieval period the *mudaraba* was the most important legal instrument for combining financial and human resources for the purposes of trade. In Islamic law and in Western commercial practice the *mudaraba* placed an indispensable role in bringing together investors and managers.

In order to avoid confusion, the students should be informed that *mudaraba* was also known as *girad* and *commenda,* the last term being used in Medieval Europe. The *mudaraba* is an arrangement in which an investor entrusts his capital or merchandise to an agent (*amil, mudarib or maqarid*), who is to trade with it and then return to the investor the principal and a previously agreed-upon share of profits. As a reward for his labor the *mudarib* receives the remaining share of the profits. Any loss resulting from the exigencies of travel or from an unsuccessful business venture is borne exclusively by the investor. The *madarib* is in no way liable for a loss of this nature, losing only his expended time and effort.[28] The complete freedom granted to the *mudarib* from any liability for the capital in the event of loss and the disjunction between the owner of capital and the third parties constitute the novel and distinctive characteristics of the *mudaraba* as well as render it particularly suitable for long-distance trade.

It has been recognized by the medievalists that the introduction of *mudaraba* into Italy during the tenth and eleventh centuries has been one of the primary factors for the expansion of medieval European trade.²⁹ Historians generally agree that the *mudaraba* was an institution indigenous to the Arabian peninsula which developed in the context of the pre-Islamic Arabian caravan trade. After the revelation, with the conquests of Islam, it spread to the Middle East, North Africa and ultimately to Southern Europe, as well as to the Far East, through transoceanic trade.

The widespread application and legitimacy of *mudaraba* is attested by the fact that Prophet Mohammed (peace be upon him), 'Umar, 'Uthman, 'Aisha all were involved one time or another in *mudaraba* transactions. Even the taxes due to the state were paid through *mudaraba:*

> The two sons of 'Umar used the provincial tax money which they were transporting to the capital of the early chalifate at Medinah as a *mudaraba,* buying Iraqi merchandise which they then sold at a profit in Medinah, and keeping half the profit for themselves and returning the original sum with the remainder of the profit to the treasury.³⁰

Sarakhsi justifies the widespread practice of *mudaraba* not only through *Sunna* but also by economic reasoning:

> *Mudaraba* is allowed because people have a need for this contract. For the owner of capital may not find his way to profitable trading activity, and the person who can find his way to such activity, may not have the capital. And profit cannot be attained except by means of both of these, that is, capital and trading activity. By permitting this contract the goal of both parties is attained.³¹

According to Abu Hanifa, a *mudaraba* contract can only be drawn with cash, i.e., gold or silver coins. "It cannot be farmed with anything except these, nor with any type of goods".³² Even copper coins were not accepted probably due to the fact that these coins (*fulus*) had limited geographical circulation. This restriction and the emphasis on wide geographical scope for the *mudaraba* is meaningful, which will become clear below when we examine the relationship between *mudaraba* and international trade. The rejection of goods and commodities for investment is basically due to two considerations which permeate the entire Islamic law of obligation. The first is the opposition to unjustified enrichment[33] and the second, its corollary, is the strict requirement that the object of any contract be determined (*ma'lum*) i.e., clearly known and defined.[34] By imposing these rejections the jurists were trying to avoid dispute and discord that may have been caused by the uncertainty of the value of goods. More importantly, they were worried about the fluctuations of the prices of these commodities which could wipe out the profit of the *mudarib* or grant him unearned and therefore (*haram*) profits. The following discussion should clarify the point:

> Why have you disapproved of this?
> He said because of the danger of his (the agent's) taking the wheat or barley and its value on the day will be 100 dirhams, and after trading with it, its value on the day he returns will be 1000 dirhams. His entire profit is thereby swallowed up. Or, its value on the day he returns it may be fifty dirhams and he will have profited from it.[35]

It should be noted that this restriction was not strictly obeyed in reality. Observing that many *mudaraba* arrangements were being farmed with investments in the form of goods and merchandise, both Hanefi and Maliki law developed a simple legal device to solve the problem—An investor may entrust goods to an agent and instruct him to sell them, and to use the cash realized from the sale as the investment in a *mudaraba* at a mutually agreed upon division of the profits. Such possibilities must have indeed nullified the force of the prohibition against goods as an investment in a *mudaraba*.

1. Industrial Mudaraba

The *mudaraba* was also quite widespread as a form of employment. Many enterprises, even the small ones, were organized in the form of *mudaraba*. This development was no doubt enhanced by the social values of the medieval era according to which dependence upon others for a livelihood (hence wage labor) was considered degrading and humiliating.[36]

Moreover, since the division of economic functions in the medieval Islamic society, though fairly advanced, was not yet complete, considerable overlappings existed between the commercial and other sectors. Therefore many *mudaraba* in which the employment of capital was associated with crafts or manufacturing were approved by the jurists. For example, a person could entrust his capital to an agent on the condition that the latter buy raw materials and process them into finished products and then sell them on the basis of shared profit. This type of arrangement which we may call industrial *mudaraba*, probably played an important role in the medieval industrialization of the Islamic world. Yet, at the existing level of our knowledge, we are not yet in a position to assess the importance of the industrial *mudaraba* at this early period.[37]

2. Mudaraba and Foreign Trade

Although most Islamic partnerships require that the cash for investment be on hand (*mal hadir*), the *mudaraba* is granted with an additional flexibility by the Hanefi school. Thus, even if the investor's capital is not on hand, but is on deposit with someone, or owed to him by another party, it is still possible to enter into a *mudaraba* agreement. This flexibility has rendered the *mudaraba* most suitable for foreign trade.

> For example, if merchant A is leaving with goods or capital for some distant point at which merchant B has an unpaid debt from C, A can be empowered to collect from C and invest in goods on a *commenda* basis for the return trip.
>
> For a creditor to ask the debtor to use the amount of money owed as a *commenda* investment is not permissible because a *commenda* cannot be formed with liable money. A *commenda* can be formed only on the basis of capital whose origin is absolutely free of liability.

Apparently, the main reason for rejecting the second type of *mudaraba* was the fear that it could lead to usury.

Under the cover of a false *commenda* agreement, the creditor could assure himself not only the recovery of his debt but also an illegal return on his loan in the guise of his share of the *commenda's* profits.[38]

One of the most important conditions for a *mudaraba* to be valid is the requirement that the control over the investment must be transferred from the investor to the *mudarib*. Indeed, requiring the *mudarib* to have clear possession of the investment and primary responsibility and authority over its disposition emphasizes one of the *mudaraba's* innovative features. Ensuring the independence of the *mudarib* and the possible anonymity of the investor vis a vis third parties have made *mudaraba* particularly suitable for long-distance trade. But this relative freedom of the *mudarib* does not imply in any way a transfer of ownership of the investment capital from the investor to the *mudarib*. While the *mudarib's* control over the disposition of investment is almost absolute, its ownership absolutely remains with the investor. It will be seen that this feature of the *mudaraba* will be of extreme importance in its modernization in the twentieth century.

In the *mudaraba* agreement the partners enjoy absolute freedom in the determination of the division of profit. There is only one requirement which is a *sine qua non* of a valid *mudaraba* contract; that the division of profit between the parties must not be in absolute amounts but in proportions. We learn from European historians that the usual profit division in medieval Italy was 3/4 profit to the investor and 1/4 to the agent.[39] On the other hand, according to the famous Geniza documents found in old Cairo, the division of profits in Medieval Egypt appears to have been much more flexible, conditioned by a wide variety of commercial and extra-commercial considerations. In the Geniza documents the following profit divisions have been observed: 1/3–2/3; 1/4–3/4; 2/5–3/5; 19/20–1/20, each one of them being legal.[40] If the condition of proportionality is violated the *mudaraba* is declared invalid.

One violation seems to have occurred rather frequently in Medieval Egypt. This is the case when one of the parties stipulates a specific sum of money from the profit instead of, or in addition to, his proportional share of the profits. Such arrangements have usually been declared as invalid by the jurists on the grounds that they could conceivably lead to a situation in which one party would get all the profit and the other none. Declaring such arrangements invalid, however, closes the way to employing the *mudarib* on a fixed wage plus profit share basis. In response to continuing demands of the merchant community the Hanefi jurists gave in and allowed this particular arrangement.[41] We will see below that this flexibility of the Hanefi jurists may enable the expansion of *mudaraba* into the industrial sector in the twentieth century.

Whatever the agreed-upon profit share may be, it is essential that this should be (*ma'lum*), clearly defined and known, by both parties. Each party's share of the profit must be clearly written down at the initiation of the contract and the designated shares should add up to the total profit.

Another noteworthy characteristic of *mudaraba* which will be of vital importance in the future expansion of the system into the modern industrial sector is the fact that multiplicity of *mudaraba,* as well as the investors, is permitted. This permission, however, is subject to the following conditions; first, as with the simple *mudaraba* i.e., with one investor and one agent, in the multiple partner *mudaraba* also it is essential that the profit shares are proportionally assigned at the initiation of the contract. Second; to avoid having one *mudarib* unjustly profit from the work of his colleague, the Maliki law insists on an equal share for each of the *mudaribs*. Third; as with the simple *Mudaraba* in multiple-partner *mudaraba* also an arrangement in which the shares of profit are not stated but left to the discretion of one of the parties at the time of the profit decision, is invalid.

In spite of the insistence of many jurists on having the profit shares fixed clearly in the contract, the Hanafi school has provided some flexibility. For instance, a *mudariba* with a flexible profit provision is permissible. The implication of this important flexibility for the foreign trade should be obvious. The basic principle here was to grant autonomy to the *mudarib* in an age of very difficult communications. Imagine for instance that two parties agree on a *mudaraba* contract to import silk to Cairo from Aleppo. The *mudarib* goes to Aleppo only to learn that he has to travel all the way to Iran in order to find silk. Since going to Iran changes the conditions of the contract altogether and since the *mudarib* has no possibility to discuss the new situation with the investor, without the flexible profit provision he would have found himself in a most difficult situation. Provision of flexible profit sharing allows the *mudarib* to make a healthy decision under such circumstances.

3. Actual Medieval Mudaraba Contracts

It may be interesting to read an actual *mudaraba* contract from the medieval era. Such a contract written by the *kadi* on behalf of the *mudarib* would read as follows:

> This is a document in favor of A son of B drawn up on the part of X son of Y which says: I have handed over to you such and such a number of dirhams of good weight in the form of a *mudaraba* on the condition that you use them to buy and sell for cash and credit in all categories of trade and in other related matters, and that you act in these matters according to your judgment. And whatsoever God, may He be exalted, grants, half of it is mine, and half of it is yours for your work. I have handed this money over to you and you have taken possession of it from me, and it amounts to such and such, in the month _____ of the year _____: it is in your possession according to what we have stated in this our document concerning this *mudaraba*.
> witnessed_____

And if the investor wishes to have a document protecting himself, again written by the *kadi*, it would read as follows:

> This is a document in favor of X son of Y drawn up by A son of B, that says: You have handed over to me such and such number of *dirhams* of good weight as a *mudaraba* on the condition that I use them to buy and sell on cash and credit in all aspects of trade, and in other related matters, and that I act in all these matters according to my judgment. And whatsoever God, may He be exalted, grants half is yours and half is mine for my work in it. You have handed over this money to me, and I have taken possession of it from you, and it amounts to such and such, in the month_____

of the year_____; and it is in my possession according to what we have stated in this our contract of this *mudaraba*. Witnessed_____.[42]

Thus the medieval *mudaraba* contract involved not one but two documents to be exchanged between the two parties. Each document contained essentially the same four elements:

1. The nature of the contract, i.e., a *mudaraba*
2. The object, i.e., the amount of the investment
3. The provisions regarding profit division and finally,
4. The *mudarib's* authorization to use it in trade as he sees fit.[43]

4. Freedom of the Mudarib

Elaboration and definition of the extent of the *mudarib's* freedom of action and clarification of his relationship with the investor and the third parties constitute a voluminous portion of the legal discussions. The following general conclusions have been drawn from these discussions[44]: Generally the *mudarib's* actions must be in conformity with the basic purpose of the contract namely, that of *achieving profit*. And they must fall within the bounds of recognized and *customary commercial practice*. But more specifically, the *mudarib's* freedom of action depends on the type of mandate he receives from the investor and on whether or not any specific conditions or limitations have been imposed at the time the contract was negotiated. With respect to the *mudarib's* activities the Hanefi law distinguished two types of contracts: a limited mandate and an unlimited mandate *mudaraba*. A *mudaraba* with an unlimited mandate is one in which the investor authorizes the *mudarib* to act completely at the latter's discretion in all business matters. The Arabic clause for this authorization being (*i'mal fihi bira' ika*) or "act with it (investment) as you see fit." In this case the *Mudarib* may:[45]

1. Buy and sell all types of merchandise as he sees fit
2. Buy and sell for cash and credit
3. Give goods as *bida'a,* leave them as a deposit or pledge
4. Hire wage laborers as needed

5. Rent or buy animals or equipment
6. Travel with the capital
7. Mingle it with his own resources (*Musharaka*)
8. Give it as a *mudaraba* to a third party
9. Invest in a partnership with a third party

It should be noted that if the clause, *l'mal fihi bira'ika* (act with it as you see fit) is not used then the *mudarib* may not engage in any of the last three items in the list, that is, he cannot mingle the investor's capital with his own resources, he cannot give it as a *mudaraba* to a third party and he cannot invest it in a partnership with a third party. But he could engage in any of the activities mentioned in the first six items of the list.

Studying the *mudaraba* practice in history, economic historians agree in general that as far as the rights of the *mudarib* is concerned it all boils down to two basic criteria: whether or not the *mudarib* has acted in order to increase the profits and whether or not he has acted in accordance with the customary practice of the merchants in the country he was visiting.

The latter criterion is particularly important in view of the competition a *mudarib* has to face from fellow merchants wherever he may have gone. If in the port he is temporarily doing his business, merchants buy their own ships to transfer their merchandise then the *mudarib* is allowed to do the same. The jurist allows him to do so through the principle of *istihsan*.[46]

It is in their conception of the scope of the *mudarib's* freedom of independent action with the *mudaraba* capital that the most important divergences appear to have occurred between the Hanefi school and the Maliki and Shafi'i schools. For the Malikis and Sharifis the *mudarib's* main task was the achievement of profit primarily by the means of buying and selling for cash. Consequently, unless specifically permitted by the investor the *mudarib* could not sell the *mudaraba* goods on credit, to accept a *hawala*[47] in payment for them, to entrust them as a *bida'a* to outside parties, etc. Therefore, engaging in any of these activities without authorization subjects the agent to liability for the entrusted capital in case of loss.

This radical differences in the attitudes of the Hanefi and Maliki schools has been explained by geographical factors. Accordingly, it has been argued that the Maliki *girad* reflected the commercial practices and needs of Medinese long-distance trade which basically took place between Mecca-Medina and Iraq/Syria in the north and Yemen in the south. The point is that no large urban centers intervened between Mecca-Medina and the termini of the trade routes mentioned above. Consequently, the structure of this trade in the first centuries of the *Hijra* must have been quite simple and straightforward—money or goods invested with a *mudarib* in Madina would be carried to Syria and Iraq, reinvested in merchandise there and in turn transported back to Medina where it would be, hopefully, resold at a profit. Thus simple buying and selling must have sufficed and the need for more complex transactions such as *ibda'a*, deposit were probably rarely felt.

By contract, the Hanefi school which flourished originally in Iraq appears to have been influenced by a vastly different economic and geographical structure. Iraq was essentially a midpoint in the vital East-West trade route between Europe and India. In the north-south direction it was again a midpoint between Central Asia and India in the East and Egypt in the west. This infinitely more complex and longer trade route interrupted frequently by major cities probably played a major role behind the relative flexibility of the Hanefi system After all, the student is reminded that Abu Hanifa himself was a silk merchant involved in international trade between Iran and Iraq.

As for the Shafi'i conception of the *mudaraba*, the emphasis here is basically on legal theory with economic considerations being rather neglected. As a result, the Shafi'i partnership is even more rigid and confined than even the Maliki *qirad*.

While touching upon the subject of international trade it should be remembered that a *mudaraba* did not automatically imply long distance. Indeed, the investor could easily put down as a condition in the contract that the *mudarib* should not travel beyond a certain city. That such a restriction had been frequently imposed by investors would be quite understandable if we consider the conditions of travel in the medieval times. For a *mudarib* doing business between Baghdad and Cairo could not, even under the best of conditions, complete his return trip at less than six months. Thus, an investor wishing to have a quick return on his capital could restrict his *mudarib* in the contract by limiting his travels only, let's say, until Aleppo.

The investor could also limit the *mudarib* in the goods that he could purchase or the persons from whom he could purchase the merchandise, etc. Yet in all these issues, in case of conflict, the basic criteria to be considered by the jurists would be the achievement of profit and the general practice of the merchants in a specific location. If, for instance, the *mudarib* has been instructed to sell for credit but he manages to sell for cash he does not become liable for the capital in his trust because he has done better than that which he was commanded. In short, any violation for the better with respect to his instructions is not a violation in the *commenda*.[48]

In the purchase and sale of goods for the *mudaraba*, the *mudarib* cannot be held responsible for any loss resulting from a reasonable use of the capital. If, however, the loss has resulted from some unreasonable transaction on the part of the *mudarib* then he is held liable. The criterion of reasonableness in this context is "that by which people will be fooled."[49] For example, if the *mudarib* spends 1000 dirhams to purchase a commodity worth only 500, he would be liable because the difference between the two prices is more than that by which people would normally be deceived. But if he used the 1000 dirhams to buy goods worth 950 dirhams he would not be held liable because this is a *"ghabn Yasir"*, a slight deception, and is a misjudgement that is easy to make.

5. The Murabaha, the Tawliya, and the Wadia

The *murabaha* which is the most common type of sale mentioned in the Jurisprudence is actually only one of the three sale types. These sale types, each starting with the cost of the sale's object to the seller, are the *tawliya*; resale at the original cost with no profit or loss to the seller; the *wadia;* resale at a discount from the original cost and the *murabaha;* the resale at fixed surcharge or rate of profit on the original cost.

According to Schacht, the exact economic functions of these institutions are not quite clear.[50] Yet, it can be argued that these institutions might have functioned as early forms of consumer protection by basing the sale price upon the original cost of the item to the seller.

This brings us to the question that just what the medieval Islamic jurists considered as cost components. There is evidence that the price paid by the seller for the goods in question, expenses connected with the maintenance, improvement and transport were considered as legitimate cost components. Consequently, the *murabaha,* for example, would be based upon a cost which combined all these components plus a certain profit on this gross cost.

What complicates our understanding the *murabaha,* however, is a later development through which the seller was allowed to declare any amount as his gross cost even if this was not in any way related to his original cost. Thus, the seller could tell to the customer, "I will sell you these commodities as a *murabaha* on the basis of three hundred dirhams and fifty dirhams profit," even though the base sum, in this case the three hundred dirhams, is far higher than his original cost.

We do not know exactly why the seller was permitted to split his gross cost from his actual cost so drastically. We can only offer speculations as an explanation, one of which may be as follows: A buyer may have been willing to pay a retailer who was at hand a surcharge on the cost of certain commodities in order to save him the trouble of obtaining them from a wholesaler who may have resided at some distance. Whatever the rationale may have been behind this permission the fact that the term *murabaha* was used at later periods in some parts of the Islamic world as an euphemism for usury indicates to the potential of misuse of this institution.[51]

We have already noted above that one of the conditions of a valid *mudaraba* is the alienation of the investor from his capital. Therefore, the *mudaraba* is initiated when the investor hands over his capital to the *mudarib*. Yet, as long as the investment is still in the form of cash the investor can exercise his option of ending the *mudaraba* or imposing further restrictions on the *mudarib's* activities. Once, however, the *mudarib* has made a purchase with the capital entrusted to him, the *mudaraba* becomes effective and the investor is not anymore allowed to interfere in the affairs of the *mudarib*. He (investor) has to wait until the *mudarib* completes his transactions and converts the capital back into cash. The interference of the investor in the affairs of the *mudarib* in this interim period would be allowed only under very special circumstances.[52]

6. The Multiple Mudaraba

Although the term *mudaraba* generally implies a commercial relationship between an investor and a *mudarib*, there is no legal opposition to a multiplicity either of investors or of agents in the same contract. In such a case the *mudaribs* are considered as one with respect to the conduct of the *mudaraba*. If an investor hands over his capital to more than one person "to act with it according to their judgement" it is understood that the *mudaribs* may act only in concert and in mutual agreement and approval. If any one of the *mudaribs* acts independently without his colleagues' permission, he becomes liable to the investor for any ensuing loss.

The only circumstances in which one agent can act without his colleagues' permission are if he obtains the investor's approval, for the permission of the investor is considered to carry at least the same weight as that of other *mudaribs*.

That a multiplicity of *mudaribs* has been allowed by the jurists may have tremendous implications for the revitalization of *mudaraba* in the twentieth century. The institution of multiple *mudaraba* may indeed open the way for a combination of *mudaraba* and the workers' management also known as the "Yugoslavian Model." Consider each worker in an industrial plant as a *madarib* and imposing on him responsibility in return for a share in the profit as well as the introduction of other characteristics of the *mudaraba* may improve the so-called "Yugoslavian Model" substantially. This is certainly an area where further research may yield most interesting results.

Another adaptation of the multiple *mudaraba* into the twentieth century is the already successful development of the Islamic banks. In this context we can consider an Islamic bank as a large investor who invests his capital with a number of *mudaribs*. The only difference with the medieval multiple *mudaraba* mentioned above is the fact that the Islamic bank considers each *mudarib* as independent of the others. However, if a modern project designed and organized by two (or more) persons is submitted to the Islamic bank then the medieval example simply repeats itself.

7. Partnership of a Muslim and Christian in a Mudaraba and the Concept of Dar-al-harb

Jurists have no objection to a Muslim acting as a *mudarib* to a Christian investor. This is allowed. The opposite case, that is, a Muslim investor entrusting his capital to a Christian *muharib* is also permitted. Yet it is considered as reprehensible for the reason that the Christian *mudarib* would not guard against usury, nor would he be fully acquainted with the basic principles of the *mudaraba*. The possibility that the Christian *mudarib* may deal in wine and pork also makes such an arrangement difficult.[53]

What has, however, made the cooperation of a Muslim and a Christian in a *mudaraba* contract really a complex problem was the concept of *dar-al-Islam* and *dar-al-harb*.[54] For it was argued that the *mudaraba* as a system of commercial cooperation could function only within those territories where Islam dominated *(Dar-al-Islam)*. Therefore, the moment a *mudarib* entered into *Dar-al-harb* while the *mudaraba* was still in force the contract became void. This was indeed a serious problem with the negative potential of ruling out any *mudaraba* designed to carry out international trade; since even if a Muslim *mudarib* carries the capital to *dar-al-harb* with the permission of the Muslim investor, the contract on the basis of legal analogy would be void. This difficult problem was solved by Hanefi jurists, probably in response to pressure of the merchants, by exercising juristic preference *(istihsan)* and thus recognizing the validity of *mudaraba* even in the *dar-al-harb*.

The tremendous contribution of this decision in the expansion of Islam should not escape us here. For it is well known that Islam spread to the far east basically through trade. Yet this trade, the carrier of Islam, was organized through the institution of *mudaraba*. Indeed, in as late as the fifteenth century every ship involved in the Malacca trade appears to have been run as a *mudaraba*. Meilink-Roelofsz explains the situation as follows:

> One thing is clear, in Asia at the end of the fifteenth century ship owning was not yet distinct from trade. The shipowner was not yet in an independent position, and the costs of transport were not yet entirely his responsibility. The captain

did not receive a salary from the people who commissioned his services, instead he shared in the profits. Nor were the members of the crew employed by the owner of the ship. They too had a share in the trade.[55]

The above description of Meilink-Roelofsz of the situation in Southeast Asia makes it quite clear that *mudaraba* was the dominant form of maritime organization.[56] Moreover, it is obvious that the type of *mudaraba* in use was the multiple mudaraba explained at the beginning of this lecture. Indeed every sailor was a *mudarib* with a share in the profits. Now, it can be hypothesized that had the Hanefi jurists not allowed the *mudaraba* to function in the *dar-al-harb* by exercising *istihsan,* the very essence of Islamic expansion, into the Far East—the maritime trade—could not have materialized for the *mudaraba* agreement between the sailors and the merchant would have become void the moment the ship left the waters of *dar-al-Islam!* It is as yet too early to reach to a conclusion on this fascinating aspect of Islamic expansion. More research is urgently needed to reveal the exact contribution of *mudaraba* as well as *istihsan* toward the Islamic expansion in the Indian Ocean.

Expenses of the *Mudarib*

Since the *mudaraba* was so closely associated with long distance travel the question of the *mudarib's* expenses assumed paramount importance. As a rule it was stipulated that the *mudarib* could deduct all legitimate expenses from the capital entrusted to him. As for the question of what exactly constituted the "legitimate" expenditure, again the twin criteria of pursuit of profit and the customary commercial practice were referred to.

The entire issue of expenses became irrelevant if the *mudarib* stayed home and did not travel. Sarakhsi has explained the rationale behind the provision of the payment of travel expenses of the *mudarib* as follows:[57] After explaining that if the *mudarib* departs with capital to another place, all his expenses can be deducted from the capital, he says:

> This is so, because of custom; for his departure and travel are on behalf of the *mudaraba* capital. A person does not normally undertake this kind of hardship for the sake of an uncertain profit which he may or may not achieve, and then pay his expenses from his own money. Because he has freed himself from all other work for the sake of the *mudaraba* capital, he is in this respect like a wife who has freed herself from all other things for the sake of her husband by staying in his house.

The jurists were so consistent in their view of the travel expenses that they carried it to its ultimate conclusion: thus even if the *mudarib* completed his journey on behalf of the *mudaraba* but did not buy any goods or invest the capital, his travel and personal expenses were still covered from the capital.

Another type of expenditure that is of interest is the bribes that the *mudarib* had to pay to government officials. According to both Abu Hanifa and Shaybani, funds spent by the *mudarib* to pay for the bribes, even for the purpose of protecting the investment from confiscation, is not to be covered from the *mudaraba* capital but from the private funds of the agent. Yet, it is interesting to note that by the eleventh century, the Hanafi position on this matter underwent a complete about face. This change obviously must have been due to the weakening of the centralized government, and the rise of uncontrolled, arbitrary power. Yet, this episode is interesting in so far as it reveals the flexible response of the jurists to changing socio-political conditions.

Another interesting type of expense occurs if the *mudarib* has been granted with an unlimited mandate *mudaraba*. In a situation like this, as we have already seen, the *mudarib* is authorized to enter into a new *mudaraba* using the funds he, himself, has been entrusted with. The question now is, if the original *mudarib* would be able to deduct the expenses of the second *mudarib* from the capital that he has been entrusted with. The answer is yes for, "In this situation he (i.e., the first *madarib*) stands in the investor's stead; and just as the first agent's expenses are borne by the capital, so too are the second agent's."[58]

9. Distribution of Liability

The most innovative feature of the *mudaraba* contract was its treatment of the distribution of liability between the parties to the contract. Accordingly, the *mudarib* was not liable for any part of the investment in case of loss. Since the *mudaraba* found its most frequent employment in long-distance trade, which by definition separated the two parties for most of the contract's duration, this distribution of liability between the parties in question was ideal.

The conception of the *mudarib* as *amin*, a trustworthy party, is the cornerstone upon which the entire structure of equity within the *mudaraba* contract rests. Any arrangement involving the *mudarib's* liability for the investment was definitely not permitted. This is because the investor was entitled to a share of the profit only by virtue of the risk of possible loss which he faced. While the *mudaraba* did entail a community of risks, the substance of each party's risk was radically different. The investor risks only his capital; the *mudarib* risks only his time and effort.[59]

It has been mentioned above that the investor is clearly separated from the third parties, that every transaction with the third parties is conducted by the *mudarib*. This implies that the investor could not be held liable for more than the amount of his original investment, i.e., the *mudarib* was not permitted to engage the *mudaraba* for any sum greater than the capital at hand. If the *mudarib* exceeded this limit in any way he would become liable for any sum in excess of the *mudaraba* capital. Naturally, the opposite was also true. That is, if he added his own funds and committed a larger capital to a venture the profits earned by this excess capital would accrue entirely to the *mudarib*. In short, beyond the limit imposed by the magnitude of the capital invested the *mudarib* was alone. The exception to this was of course the case when the investor authorized the *mudarib* to incur debts in excess of the amount of *mudaraba*.

10. Conclusion of the Mudaraba

Just as the *mudaraba* could not commence without the investor relinquishing control over his capital and handing it over to the *mudarib*, so too, did its conclusion depend on the agent's restoring it to the investor, the exact amount being restored depending upon the success of the *mudaraba*. Other than by means of such "natural" conclusion there were a number of provisions which ended a *mudaraba*. These were: the decision of either party to withdraw; the death; the insanity; or apostasy from Islam of either party. In such cases (excluding the apostasy which has its own rules) the *madaraba* was dissolved by immediately converting all its assets into cash, by restoring the capital to the investor (or his heirs), and dividing the remainder, if any, among the parties according to the agreement.

We have studied until now the structure of the *mudaraba* during the first three centuries of Islam. At the almost total absence of archival materials, which could have allowed us to observe the actual practice in daily commercial transactions, we were forced to rely on legal writings emanating from this period. At this point it is therefore appropriate to ask whether these legal texts reflect the actual life. The question has been answered by the leading authorities affirmatively, particularly with reference to the Hanefi school.[60] These scholars argue that the institution of *istihsan* (juristic preference) enabled the Hanefi jurists to respond quite flexibly to the demands and problems of the commercial community. Hence the Hanefi, particularly, but to a lesser extent also Maliki and Shari'i legal writings adequately reflect the actual commercial practice during the medieval era.

This leads us immediately into the next question: What happened to the institution of *mudaraba* after the medieval era? Did it survive, or die? Was it abandoned? Or did it continue to flourish? If it did flourish, in what ways did it change in response to the relentless pressures of the times? We will examine these questions below.

VII

The *Mudaraba* in the Early Modern Period

We had concluded our last lecture with a set of questions concerning the fate of the *mudaraba* in the post-medieval period. These questions were the following:

> What happened to the institution of *mudaraba* after the medieval era? Did it survive or die? Was it abandoned? Or did it continue to flourish? If it did flourish, in what ways did it change in response to the relentless pressures of the times?

This lecture will address itself to these questions.

1. Sources

Unlike the medieval period, for later periods we are privileged to have vast amounts of historical sources which can be of inestimable value for answering the questions mentioned above. Yet, the almost total disinterest of the Muslim historians with these later periods has resulted in a paucity of knowledge that is simply unpardonable.

In Cairo and Istanbul there are immensely rich archives which have *never* been searched with the questions posted above in mind. Only a few historians, so far as I know, have searched for the financial techniques prevailing in the later periods, and all of them concentrated their research on small Ottoman towns of secondary importance. The largest of these towns, Bursa, has a relatively small archive of 800 volumes of Sharia Court Registers. By comparison, the archives of the office of Mufti of Istanbul contain 10,000 volumes!!! This is, of course, excluding the Topkapi Palace archives and, particularly, the Prime Ministry Archives with 400 million documents! In short, a detailed history of the Islamic financial history in the later periods can be written, yet, for the time being, we are limited by only a few articles mentioned below.[61]

The nature of the documents contained in the Ottoman archives is such that even these four articles have succeeded in destroying old prejudices and have forced historians to have a completely new look on Islamic financial history. This point needs to be elaborated.

2. Islamic Financial Law in Practice

The founding fathers of Oriental studies in the West were of the opinion that the *fiqh* had very little to do with actual practice. It was only of theoretical significance for it was developed by jurists according to the paradigm of the golden age, i.e., the period of the first four caliphs.

The religious-legal scholars endeavored to create an ideal doctrine of how things ought to be, yet the things were not at all as they ought to be.[62] That legal theory was designed by jurists in their ivory towers and never found application was also suggested by Hurgronje in the following words:

> All classes of the Muslim community have exhibited in practice an indifference to the sacred law in all its fulness, quite equal to the reverence with which they regard it in theory.[63]

In short, according to these early Orientalists, one could study *fiqh* only for its own sake without trying to link it to the actual practice, for its contents, with the possible exception of the first two centuries of Islam, never found application in real life.

This rather negative view was seriously challenged first by Abraham Udovitch of Princeton University. Benefiting from the massive amount of work done by Goitein in the recently discovered Geniza archives of Cairo, he observed that bulk of the principles laid down by early jurists during the seventh and eighth centuries found widespread application in Cairo during the eleventh and twelfth centuries.[64] Moreover, according to Udovitch and Goltein,[65] the application of these principles were so well-established and widespread that even the Jews preferred to deal in Islamic *mudaraba* rather than the less flexible Talmudic *'isqa*.[66] Hence, the link between *fiqh* and reality was established.

Yet, even Udovitch was firmly convinced that the Islamic financial institutions he has described throughout his book did not survive the Middle Ages. In the very last sentence of his book he makes the following statement:

> The efficacy and vitality of these legal-commercial institutions endured, I believe, for most of the Islamic Middle Ages.[67]

3. Mudaraba in the Seventeenth Century

In a ten-page article based upon his studies in the Sharia Court Registers of Bursa, it was Haim Gerber, an Israeli scholar of Hebrew University, who proved that the *mudaraba* was well and alive as late as the seventeenth century.[68] Concerning, for instance, the *mudaraba* Gerber has made the following observations:

> Studying the *kadi* records of seventeenth century Anatolian Bursa we have found no less than ninety references to business partnerships.... What is important is the fact that there was a free use of the orthodox Islamic partnership.... Thus, in a case brought before the *kadi* of Bursa in 1693 the decision began with the words: "Reference was made to the fikh books."[69] And in one document relating to a *mudaraba* partnership from 1671 a distinction is made between the investor and the agent; it is specified that the investor gets 2/3 of the profits and the agent 1/3, and it is explained that the

> agent is supposed to follow exactly the investor's directions. And these are some of the most important ingredients of the law of partnership in classical Islam. In yet another example, a *commenda* agent, in the name of the partnership incurred liabilities amounting to more than the sum invested in the partnership. Such an act is called by classical Islamic law *istidana,* and is illegal without the express consent of the investor. Indeed, in the case from 1682, where such a dispute was brought to court, the agent lost the case on the basis of the saying: "The *istidana* is illegal without approval." It is thus evident that the court paid meticulous attention to the classical law of partnership.
>
> From the ninety or so partnerships found in the kadi records of the seventeenth-century Bursa, thirty-two were of the *mudaraba* type; ten were of the *mufawada* type; six were *inan,* two *sanai* and two were of the *vucuh* type. All the rest were simply described as Sirket, that is, partnership, with no further specification. . . . From the statistics presented above it looks as if the *commenda* (*mudaraba*) partnership was the most important type of partnership in seventeenth-century Bursa.[70]

This long quotation needs no further comment. I should perhaps, only add that bursa Court Registers revealed clearly that in seventeenth-century Turkey as in Medieval Egypt, the *mudaraba* was used particularly in long-distance trade (importation of coffee and silk into Bursa from Yemen and Iran).

Moreover, Muslims and Christians did draw *mudaraba* contracts. The *mudaraba,* apparently was also utilized to maintain permanent business relations between merchants living in two different cities, one between Bursa and Aleppo and the other between Bursa and Istanbul. The *mufawada* and *inan* partnerships were mainly used, as might be expected, in small local business.

In order to appreciate the significance of the next case discovered by Gerber, I have to quote myself; talking about the *multiple mudaraba* and its possible application to the industry I have said in the last lecture:

That a multiplicity of *mudaribs* has been allowed by the jurists may have tremendous implications for the revitalization of *mudaraba* in the twentieth century. The institution of *multiple mudaraba* may indeed open the way for a combination of *mudaraba* and the workers' management, also known as the "Yugoslavian Model."

Well, it seems we neither have to "wait" until the twentieth century nor have to take the so-called "Yugoslavian Model" as an example. For, in seventeenth-century Bursa, the *multiple mudaraba* was used in the industry successfully, with workers managing themselves as responsible *mudaribs* and sharing their profits with the investors! This fascinating event occurred in 1678 when the cottoncarder's guild of Bursa faced an unexpected tax demand by the Ottoman government, pressed by the financial demands of the 1672–81 Russo-Turkish war. Two enterprising members of the guild volunteered to act as investors in a *mudaraba* agreement. Accordingly, they undertook to pay the taxes due to the guild in return for the entire production of the guild for that year. The agreement was a typical multiple *mudaraba* for the investors sold the total produce in the market and after compensating themselves for the taxes which they paid fully, they split the profit between themselves and the *mudaribs,* each one of whom was a fellow guild member.[71]

To conclude this lecture, the examples and cases presented above answer adequately the first four questions which we have asked at the beginning of this lecture. Thanks to the recent research summarized above we now know that the *mudaraba* survived the Middle Ages. It was certainly not abandoned by the Muslim empires of the post medieval era.[72] And, perhaps, equally importantly, the *mudaraba* not merely survived but was successfully applied to different sectors. Obviously, it may be considered as dangerous to reach to such general conclusions based upon the limited work that has been done so far. Nevertheless, the findings and the sources upon which they are based are such that, it seems, to continue to insist that the *mudaraba* died at the end of the medieval era would be even more dangerous.

In the next lecture we will study the newer forms of *mudaraba* that are not known in the classical legal sources as well as the further survival of this remarkable institution into the nineteenth and twentieth centuries.

4. Various Applications of Mudaraba in the Seventeenth Century

In the last lecture I have presented the results of the latest research as evidence which proved that the *mudaraba* survived the Middle Ages and was applied for a variety of purposes in seventeenth century Ottoman Bursa. Having rediscovered this institution six, seven hundred years later than when it was last observed, one cannot help but wonder if and in what ways the *mudaraba* has changed in this period. Gerber's work provides us with information also concerning this question.

> The *sicil* of seventeenth-century Bursa shows the free use, in the court, of legal arrangements and contracts which are new and unknown to the *Sharia*. Such, for example, was the case of the *istiglal* which was an arrangement for lending money on interest in lieu of a mortgage of real estate.[73]

Moreover, apparently, some classical Islamic institutions changed their meaning and were used in the seventeenth century for different purposes. For example, the institution of *musaka,* which meant in the medieval era a lease contract of agricultural land where the produce was divided between the two parties in a Sharecropping agreement, was used in a totally different way in the seventeenth-century Bursa.

In Bursa, the *musaka* was an arrangement whereby *wakf* property was alienated to an individual for a long period through leasing. The division of the property was such that the lessee would get 99 percent of the produce and the *wakf* 1 percent. Even this 1 percent was to accrue to the lessee who would "maintain" the property. Gerber's comment on this observation is simply the following; "The arrangement has thus little resemblance to the Islamic *musaka*. There is no trace of these new legal institutions in the famous guidebooks."

Actually, it is not at all surprising that the seventeenth-century *musaka* cannot be found in the classical legal texts. This is for the probable reason that in the seventeenth-century *musaka* we are observing an institution which facilitated the transition from the classical Ottoman system of land tenure into the system of private ownership of land. We will discuss these problems in detail in the future lectures.

VIII

Mudaraba in the Nineteenth and Twentieth Centuries

The evidence for the survival of *mudaraba* in these very recent times, in this case, in rural Palestine, has been provided by Ya'akov Firestone.[74] Based upon private records of some Palestinian families and as well as on oral history, Firestone has proved that in the period 1853–1943 the institution of *mudaraba* was again healthy and doing well. Moreover, the *mudaraba* was not the only Islamic institution that had survived. Other agricultural partnerships such as the *muzara'a* (co-cultivation between landlord and grain-growing peasant), the *musaka* (the agreement for tending and irrigation between horticulturist and cultivator)[75] the *mugharasa* (the planting contract between grove owner and worker) were also very much alive and found application.

Concerning the *mudaraba*, Firestone has observed nine cases during the short period of five years, between 1853–1858. This point must be elaborated.

That, the collection of Hamdan family which extends over a period of seventy years, contains a few yet solid evidence on the existence of *mudaraba* for only five years must be explained. Indeed, why does the *mudaraba* suddenly appear in this short period, only to disappear again equally suddenly? The explanation is found in the political events dominating those years.

The period 1853–1858 corresponds to the famous Crimean War during which the Allied forces of Britain and France helped the

Ottomans to stop Russian advance to the south. The demand for foodstuffs of this combined force of about half a million men was immediately felt all over the Ottoman empire. Rural Palestine was no exception. There is nothing extraordinary in this story so far. But what is extraordinary is the speed with which a relatively isolated area like the landlocked reaches of the Palestine hills responded to the new demand AND even more importantly, they used the *mudaraba* for this purpose.

The implications should be clear; first, the population of rural Palestine always knew about the *mudaraba* but they did not utilize it as long as they remained a self-sufficient community. Second, as soon as the war demand was felt, the *mudaraba* was taken out of its mothballs and vigorously utilized. All of this should prove beyond any doubt the extraordinary suitability of this remarkable institution to the foreign trade. The strength of the correlation between foreign trade and the *mudaraba* can also be observed in the following table.[76]

Year	Value of exports from Beirut to England (E)	Commenda holdings of Mahmoud Abdurrazzaq and his brothers (PT)
1854	29.833	4.500
1855	96.534	15.000
1856	42.765	7.500
1857	66.912	8.250
1858	31.348	8.000
1859	8.052	3.000

The table, indeed, demonstrates most clearly the amazing harmony between the value of total exports and the total *mudaraba* holdings of the family in question. It is also noteworthy that the *mudaraba contracts yielded the family 20–30 percent net return annually which was far in excess of alternative investment possibilities including interest-bearing loans.*[77]

The next question that comes to mind is: whether or not the *mudaraba* has not changed substantially in this region from its classical ancestor. To answer this question Firestone has grouped the nine deeds into two groups: The first group of contracts were drawn in the first half of the period, i.e., 1853–1856. These contracts are so loyal to the classical examples that they could just as well have been written in the year 1053 instead of 1853. There is one clause in these contracts which, however, has puzzled Professor Firestone. Consider the following sentence; "Half of the sum (the amount given by the investor to the entrepreneur) was received as a loan and the other half in *commenda* (*girad*)."[78] Apparently, the five contracts drawn in the next period also contain a sentence about half the sum being remitted as a loan and half in *mudaraba*. Firestone, totally confused, has asked, "What, then, has happened here?" without providing a convincing answer. Yet this particular type of *mudaraba* has been explained very clearly by Udovitch as follows:

> The Hanafis do permit what might be described as a mixed investment, i.e., an arrangement whereby the investor entrusts a given sum of money to an agent, half or any other fraction of which is a *commenda* investment, and the remainder either a loan, deposit, or *ibda*. It would seem that the purpose of such arrangements was to extend the possible variations in the distribution of profits and risks. By conferring the status of loan on part of the sum, the investor enjoys greater security with respect to his capital. The agent is liable under all circumstances for the return of that portion. But by the same token, the investor is reducing his prospects for profit by a similar fraction. . . . Employment of these hybrid arrangements were probably a function of market conditions.[79]

Thus, there is no reason for being confused, what we are observing in nineteenth-century Palestine is a specific type of *mudaraba* also observed in the Middle Ages.

In the next group, however, one deviation from the classical *mudaraba* has been observed. These are the four contracts which stipulate that the losses will be divided among the parties in the same proportion as profits.[80] As it is well known, in the classical *mudaraba* profits are divided between the partners according to a previously agreed-upon share. Yet, the loss accrues to the investor alone, the loss of the *mudarib* being in the nature of unrewarded work and effort. Why one of these essential principles of the classical *mudaraba* was violated in these cases in the nineteenth-century Palestine is not clear. We need extensive research to enlighten us on this puzzle.

1. Mudaraba in Agriculture

a. Tunisia

Up to now I have stressed the perfect adjustment of the *mudaraba* into foreign trade. This should, however, not mislead us to the wrong impression that the *mudaraba* was not used for other purposes. Indeed, we have solid evidence, from nineteenth-century Tunisia, that the *mudaraba* was also extensively used in agriculture.[81]

In Tunisia it was known as *Qirad* and was applied in livestock raising. Tunisian evidence supports the point made above based upon the Palestinian experience concerning the close relationship between the *mudaraba* and overall political-economic conditions. Apparently, in Tunisia, it was the relative safety provided to North Africa by the French occupation as well as the demand for foodstuffs by these foreign troops which revitalized the *Mudaraba*. One cannot but help noticing the irony of this situation; whereby European occupation ends up revitalizing an ancient Islamic institution! In the Tunisian *Qirad* the *muqarid* raised and bred a herd or flock for an investor in return for a share in the produce and the increase. This type of *qirad*, to be sure, constitutes a deviation from the classical *qirad*, in the sense that the latter can only be formed by cash. Yet, apparently, under the nineteenth-century Ottoman civil code, the *mejelle*, a solution, has been found for this by having each partner sell half of his property to the other.[82]

b. Palestine (twentieth century)

Returning to Palestine, we observe that the *mudaraba* was also used in livestock raising in this region. The emergence of the *mudaraba* in the Ya'bad forest under the Mandate bears striking resemblance to the emergence of the Tunisian *qirad* in livestock raising. The provision of peace and order, this time by the British, under the Magnate (1923–1948) as well as the market activated by foreign colonization appear to have been the main forces behind the revitalization of the *mudaraba* in the Palestinian countryside. Firestone describes the Palestinian agricultural *mudaraba* as follows:

> An investor—usually a cheese merchant from Ya'bad—would select a likely *sharik* (*mudarib*) from among the dwellers in the forest or the vicinity, buy a herd of goats for him to tend, and assign him a share of its value. A starting share was usually one-fourth or one-third of the assessed worth of the herd, and a note was drawn up in the amount. The entrepreneur was to return this debt to the investor within a specified period ranging generally from three to five years.
>
> Each year, when the male kids and the culls were sold, the proceeds were reinvested in the herd or divided among the parties in proportion to their agreed charter shares in the capital. The females were retained for increase. When the *Sharika* was terminated, the herd was partitioned. It was not possible for either party to sell any of the stock on account of its share alone without dissolving the *Sharika*.
>
> The entrepreneur took the entire produce of the herd for himself, as well as the goat hair, in compensation for his toil.[83]

In the 1930s another development was instrumental in the further expansion of the *mudaraba* in livestock raising. This was the expansion of the cultivated land as well as fruit growing at the expense of the husbandman's pasture preserve. Consequently, the latter was driven to remoter and remoter districts. Yet, at the same time the market demand for livestock products was expanding. In short, husbandmen found themselves in a situation where they were being pushed farther and farther away by an increasingly lucrative market. How they reacted to this is revealed by a few oral case histories obtained by Firestone from the village of Arrabch:

> Mahmud, who took over part of his father's property at the time, accordingly, concluded *sharika* agreements with

two men from neighboring hamlets. We shall follow one of them. It involved fifty head valued at £P 75, of which the herdsman (*mudarib*) Muhammed Yusuf Abu Jalbush of the neighboring hamlet of Mirka, was debited half, to be paid up in three annual installments. As in the *sharika* contracts current at the time in the Ya'bad district, the increase was to be divided half and half and the produce was to go to Muhammad in its entirety.

Muhammed met his payments each year; in fact having a number of sons who could herd, he was interested in increasing the flock faster than the sheep multiplied, and he came to Mahmud a few times for a few pounds as the investor's half share in additional acquisitions. In his account of this, Mahmud stressed the fiduciary nature of the relationship (*amanah*; i.e., trust, as he called it) by volunteering that at no time did he ask Muhammed how many sheep there now were in the flock, or even how many he intended to buy with the money he was asking.

In four years the flock grew from fifty to 140 head.... The *sharika* was formally partitioned, whereupon Muhammed sold his half of the stock back to Mahmud at £P1.500 per head.[84]

This fascinating story invites several comments.

1. Despite the different terminology used by Firestone it is obvious that we are dealing with a *mudaraba* of, what Udovitch calls, the "mixed investment" type.
2. Since the capital was in kind and not in cash, we are observing a deviation, the only one, from the classical *mudaraba*.
3. The tremendous increase in the price must have been due to monetary (inflation) as well as real causes, i.e., the socio-political conditions described above.
4. I have calculated the rate of profit for each partner as 5500 percent!!! May I suggest that the future Islamic Bankers make a note of this?

IX

Conclusion

1. Mudaraba and Banking

At the beginning of this course we have seen that the deposit banking, an institution of supreme importance for the economic development of the West, did not emerge in the Islamic world. The basic function of this institution was to bring the small savings of many savers at the service of the entrepreneurs, thus channeling savings into investment, hence, facilitating economic development.

We have also seen that the basic function of these deposit banks, i.e., bringing together the saver and the entrepreneur, was fulfilled by the institution of *mudaraba* in the Islamic world. As a matter of fact, there is overwhelming evidence that the *mudaraba* functioned much more smoothly and efficiently than the Western deposit banking—bank failures were unknown in the Islamic world. Moreover, as latest research has demonstrated, the *mudaraba* had as much, if not more, staying power as the deposit banking.

2. Paradox of the Mudaraba

There was, however, one weakness associated with the *mudaraba;* although it functioned smoothly, it was basically dependent upon a thorough acquaintance of the two partners. It could only function if each partner knew the other very well. As a result of this, the scale of economic activities in the Islamic world was necessarily limited to numerous small, even intimate, circles. Consequently, the massive volume of private investment generated by the Western deposit banking could not materialize in the Islamic world, leading to the sad consequences that we all know.

3. Islamic Banking

It is in this context that we must view the tremendous potential of modern Islamic banking. In my opinion, the greatest potential contribution of Islamic banking lies in the fact that, for the first time in Islamic economic history, a perfectly functioning yet an informal and necessarily small-scale institution may be transformed into a formal, large-scale body with unlimited growth potential hence dissolving the paradox of *mudaraba*.

This transformation will probably occur by an ingenious combination of some of the features of the *mudaraba*. Namely, the multiple *mudaraba* in combination with the principle of complete autonomy of the *mudarib* vis a vis the third parties. I have indicated above that there is no legal opposition to a multiplicity either of investors or of *mudaribs* in the same contract. The modern Islamic bank can be viewed as a *mudarib* dealing with many (hopefully millions) of investors, in this case small savers as in the case of Western deposit banking. This is the first tier of the modern Islamic bank. The second tier involves the Islamic bank as a major investor dealing with many *mudaribs* i.e., the firms financed by the bank.

In this triple arrangement (i.e. savers, Islamic bank and firms) which we may call the triple mudaraba, the autonomy of the original *mudarib* (Islamic bank) vis a vis the third parties (firms) is, of course, indispensable. In fact, without this principle, an Islamic bank would simply be unthinkable.

The greatest challenge to the world of Islamic commerce in the twentieth century is, I believe, to transform the classical *mudaraba*, into an equally smooth functioning and efficient modern Islamic bank with the potential of almost unlimited growth. This is the task of Islamic bankers!

EPILOGUE

Too Much of a Good Thing[85]

They are the conduits of a latter-day California gold rush: one Silicon Valley address, in Menlo Park, Calif., lists twenty-seven venture capital firms. Hoping to strike it rich and match the dazzling success of early winners like Apple Computer, they have poured well over $1 billion into new high-technology start-up companies in the past two years. But the tidal wave of venture capital is turning out to be a mixed blessing. 'Ultimately, all that capital speeds up the consolidation of the industry,' says analyst Peter Wright of the Gartner Group. "That's what we see happening right now."
The big problem is that the stampede of venture capitalists and investors has made it almost too easy to start new companies.

"There's never been more cash available," says James Lally of Kleine, Perkins, Caufield & Byers, a San Francisco venture-capital firm. "As a result, a whole series of 'me-too' companies have been started. They are developing products that do not have a unique feature or competitive advantage. They don't stand a chance."

The flood of venture capital also helps speed up product cycles; the meteoric rise of Osborne Computer lasted only fifteen months before sales faltered. In the supercharged market, companies that don't keep up or don't have the financial resources to endure mistakes are swiftly brought down. "Many companies are not prepared to face a long-term capital drain," says analyst Alexander Stein of Dataquest. "They are not looking that far ahead."

Moving on: The shakeout in the personal-computer market has had a sobering effect on investors who thought they couldn't lose by betting on high technology. Many are new players who got caught in markets they apparently did not understand. The venture capitalists' game has always been a gamble, but the savviest players try to cut the odds. For many firms that means avoiding the personal and home computer markets and investing instead in computer software and peripherals, computer-aided design and manufacturing systems, semiconductors, robotics and medical technology.

"Venture capital has already moved on to other markets," says Gib Myers of the Mayfield Fund, a venture-capital firm in Menlo Park, Calif. "The money is still out there."

That little article provoked my thoughts in the following directions:

1. The West seems to be at it again! That is, the business of borrowing from the East and then dominating the East with what they have borrowed! The Americans have discovered the *mudaraba* (just as the Italians did in the Middle Ages) and seem to be pleased with it!
2. In an age of high-interest rates with conventional banks financing only short-term loans, the *mudaraba* will probably save the American industry from financial starvation. So they have every reason to be pleased with this "good thing".
3. The fact that the most promising, dynamic and advanced-technology sector of the American economy is financed through the *mudaraba* proves the incredible adoptability and *modernity* of this institution.
4. Since Americans feel perfectly free about borrowing our heritage we should feel equally free about doing the same. That is, if they have invented new arrangements in adopting the *mudaraba* into modern business we should by all means study and adopt them, providing they are in conformity with Islamic principles.
5. Without developing needless complexes we should also benefit from the American experience by observing very carefully the problems they are having and reformulate our economic theories. For instance, Islamic economists have been arguing that in the future Islamic economy the business cycles will be curbed by the institution of *zekat*. In Silicon Valley, however, "The flood

of venture capital helps speed up product cycles." This should be taken as a warning; the incredible dynamism of the *mudaraba* may easily overshadow the curbing effect of the *zekat!* Indeed, the American problem with the "good thing" appears to be neither the shortage of capital nor the entrepreneurs but rather that "the stampede of venture capitalists and inventors has made it almost too easy to start new companies." Consequently, the economists are seriously worried that too many companies, too much competition will lead to a rather painful process of elimination in this sector.

6. The instinct of the American businessmen combined with the flexibility of the *mudaraba* appear to be solving this problem. Indeed the *Newsweek* reports: "Venture capital has already moved on to other markets." Thus, we should not be surprised at all if the *mudaraba* ends up dominating the bulk of the American business scene in the future.

7. *Newsweek* reports: "There has never been more cash available." Thus, the modern *mudaraba* appears, finally, to be solving the paradox of the classical *mudaraba*, that is, savings are channeled into investments.

8. Finally, the amazing success of *our mudaraba* in the last quarter of the twentieth century in the most advanced sector of the most advanced economy of the world, should convince us of the future and potential of Islamic banking, in our countries. We would not be worth our religion and heritage if we fail in this challenge of achieving economic development through Islamic banking.

NOTES

1. J. Hicks, *A Theory of Economic History*, (Oxford: Clarendon Press, 1969), p. 78.
2. Robert S. Lopez, "The Dawn of Medieval Banking", *The Dawn of Modern Banking* ed. by Center for Medieval and Renaissance Studies, U.C.L.A. (London: Yale U. Press, 1979), p. 1.
3. Fritz M. Heichelheim, *An Ancient Economic History*, (Leiden: Brill, 1958, 1964), 2 volumes, *passim*.
4. For an excellent summary of medieval Italian banking see; Raymond de Roover, "New Interpretations of the History of Banking", *Journal of World History*, vol. II, 1954, pp. 38–76.
5. A. L. Udovitch, "At the origins of the Western *Commenda*: Islam, Israel, Byzantium?", *Speculum*, XXXVII, 2 (April 1962). See particularly the section on *"Qirad* and *Commenda"*.
6. Sidney Homer, *A History of Interest Rates*, (New Brunswick: Rutgers University Press, 1963), p. 76.
7. Andre E. Sayous, "Les Operations des Tanquiers Italiens an Italie et aux Foires de Champagne Pendant le XIII Siecle", *Revue Historique* CLXX (1932), p. 6.
8. Raymond De Roover, *Money Banking and Credit in Medieval Brugge* (Cambridge, Mass.: The Medieval Academy of America, 1948), p. 263.
9. Raymond De Roover, "New Interpretations . . .", p. 43.
10. J. Le Goff, "The Usurer and the Purgatory", *The Dawn of Modern Banking*, p. 52.
11. Sidney Homer, *A History of Interest Rates*, pp. 79–81.
12. Frederic C. Lane, "Venetian Bankers, 1496-1533; A Study in the Early Stages of Deposit Banking", *The Journal of Political Economy*, XLV (1937), p. 187.
13. During the Turco-Venetian wars of 1650 and 1714–1739.
14. Pierre Vilar, *A History of Gold and Money*, (London: NLB, 1976), p. 230.

15 A. Birnie, *An Economic History of Europe 1760–1939* (London: Methuen, 1962 repr.), ch. 6.
16 Traute Wohlers-Scharf, *Arab and Islamic Banks, New Business Partners for Developing Countries,* (Paris: O.E.C.D. report, 1983), Part II.
17 Raymond de Roover, "New Interpretations . . .", p. 43.
18 Abraham L. Udovitch, "Bankers without Banks: Commerce, Banking, and Society in the Islamic World of the Middle Ages", *Dawn of Modern Banking,* (Yale University Press, 1979), pp. 255–273.
19 Charles Issawi, (ed.), *The Economic History of the Middle East, 1600–1914.* (Chicago: Chicago University Press, 1966), pp. 10–11.
20 A possible exception to this statement may have been the Ottoman institution of *Cash Vakfs*. On the tremendous controversy and debate between the Ottoman *Ulema* on this subject see; J.E. Mandaville, "Usurious Piety: The Cash Waqf Controversy in the Ottoman Empire", *International Journal of Middle East Studies,* vol. 10, 1979, No. 3, pp. 299–308.
21 I. Goldziher, J. Schacht and M. Rodinson represent this school of thought.
22 A.L. Udovitch, "Bankers without Banks", p. 258.
23 A.L. Udovitch, "Bankers without Banks", p. 258.
24 Perhaps, in view of the system of Islamic land tenure and the resulting system of income distribution this outcome was inevitable. In Islamic economics the masses in the agricultural sector were not in a position to save. Saving, instead, was done by the state and the members of the ruling class. In the West, relatively early development of the private ownership of land as well as the organized opposition of the masses against excessive taxation enabled the masses to save.
25 A.L. Udovitch, "Bankers without Banks", p. 262. Also notice the respect paid and full recognition of the concept of profit by the Islamic jurists.
26 *Ibid.,* p. 264. (Kasani quoted by Udovitch).
27 S. Homer, *A History of Interest Rates,* p. 78.
28 This description has been adopted with minor changes from A.L. Udovitch, *Partnership and Profit in Medieval Islam,* (Princeton: Princeton University Press, 1970) p. 170.
29 R.S. Lopez and I.W. Raymond, *Medieval Trade in the Mediterranean World* (London: 1961).
30 Sarakhsi, *Mabsut,* 22:18, quoted by Udovitch, *Partnership and Profit,* p. 173.
31 *Ibid.,* p. 175.
32 *Ibid.,* p. 177.
33 J. Schacht, *An Introduction to Islamic Law,* (Oxford: Oxford University Press, 1964), p. 144.

34 *Ibid.*, p. 147.
35 Discussion between Sahnun and Abd' ar-Rahman b. Al Kasim quoted by A.L. Udovitch, *Partnership and Profit*, p. 181.
36 S.D. Goitein, *A Mediterranean Society*, (Berkeley/Los Angeles: University of California Press, 1967), vol., I, p. 92ff.
37 Rejection of the industrial *mudaraba* by the Maliki and Shafi'i schools may have undermined its impact on industrial expansion. These schools preferred to consider the *mudaraba* purely as a commercial instrument. Industrial *mudaraba* was approved by the Hanefi School.
38 A.L. Udovitch, *Profit and Partnership*, pp. 187–188.
39 R.S. Lopez and I.W. Raymond, *Medieval Trade in the Mediterranean World*, (London: 1961), p. 175.
40 S.D. Goitein, *A Mediterranean Society*, p. 174. For *mudaraba* being practiced by medieval Jewish bankers see; S.D. Goitein, "Bankers' Accounts from the Eleventh Century A.D.", *Journal of the Economic and Social History of the Orient*, vol. IX, 1966.
41 The Hanefi permission was indirect: The investor hires an agent to carry on trade in return for a fixed wage and entrusts to him the necessary capital to do so. The agent then gives the funds to the investor on a *mudaraba* basis; the investor then returns them to the agent as *bida'a*. The agent, thus, continues to receive his fixed wage plus a share of the commenda profit. *Bida'a/Ibda'*: Type of informal commercial collaboration in which one party entrusts his goods to the care of another to be sold after which the latter without any compensation, profit or commission returns the proceeds of the transaction to the first party. Definition by A.L. Udovitch, *op. cit.*, p. 273.
42 A.L. Udovitch, *Partnership and Profit*, p. 197, 198.
43 For further details on the order of clauses and formulae etc. in the medieval Arabic documents see; A.J. Wakin, *Islamic Law in Practice*, (New York: Columbia University dissertation, 1968).
44 A.L. Udovitch, *op. cit.*, p. 204.
45 A.L. Udovitch, *op. cit.*, p. 204.
46 *Istihsan:* Juristic preference in Hanefi law, an exercise of discretionary opinion in breach of strict analogy. Definition; Udovitch, *op. cit.*, p. 274.
47 Hawala: Transfer of debt.
48 Sarakhsi, *Mabsut*, 22:44 quoted by Odovitch, *op. cit.*, p. 214.
49 Shaybani, *Asl*, Mudaraba, quoted by Udovitch, *op. cit.*, p. 216.
50 J. Schacht, *An Introduction to Islamic Law*, (Oxford, Oxford University Press, 1964), pp. 152–154 also see *id.*, (ed.) *G. Bergstrasser's Grundzuge des Islamischen*

Rechts (Berlin, 1935), pp. 71–72.

51 In the late sixteenth century the "murabahacilar", i.e., those who engage in *murabaha* in Anatolia were exiled to Cyprus. Problem of restocking faced by retailers, particularly in inflationary periods was probably a more important concern prompting such practices. Under inflation, a retailer is forced to increase his prices continuously, if he is to be able to restock his shop. Indeed his original cost may have been only 150 but if he did not sell at 300 plus profit he simply would not have the cash to pay the current price in the market (300) when he has to restock.

52 For details see, A.L. Udovitch, *op. cit.,* p. 223.

53 It is interesting to note in this context that the Muslim jurists have disregarded here the similar prohibition of usury by the church.

54 *Dar-al-Islam:* Lands of Islam.
Dar-al-harb: Literally the domain of war, i.e., countries where Islam was rejected.
Harbi: A person from the *dar-al-harb.*

55 Melink-Roelofsz, "Trade and Islam in the Malay-Indonesian Archipelago Prior to the Arrival of the Europeans," in *Islam and the Trade of Asia* ed. By D.S. Richards, (Oxford: Bruno Cassier/University of Pennsylvania Press, 1970), pp. 151–152.

56 Tome Pires, the Portuguese government accountant in Malaca, was much more direct when he described these maritime arrangements—He called them simply the *commenda.* See, Tome Pires, *Suma Oriental* vol. II, pp. 283–85.

57 Quoted by A.L. Udovitch, *op. cit.,* p. 231, 232.

58 Quoting from Sarakhasi, *Mabsut,* 22:66, A.L. Udovitch, *op. cit.,* p. 237.

59 A.L. Udovitch, *op. cit.,* p. 240.

60 A.L. Udovitch, *op. cit.,* p. 250.

61 Ronald C. Jennings "Loans and Credits in early 17th Century Ottoman Judicial Records", *Journal of the Economic and Social History of the Orient,* vol. XVI (1973), p. 168–216, of particular importance is; Haim Gerber, "The Muslim Law of Partnerships in Ottoman Court Records", *Studia Islamica* vol. LIII, pp. 109–119 and, Ya'akov Firestone, "Production and Trade in an Islamic Context", *International Journal of Middle East Studies,* vol. 6 (1975) pp. 185–209. Also see; H. Sahillioglu, "Bursa Kadi Sicillerinde ic ve Dis odemeler Araci olark 'Kitab-ul' Kadi ve 'sufteceler'", *Turkiye iktisat Tarihi Semineri* (ed.). O. Okyar, (Ankara: Hacettepe Un., 1975).

62 I. Goldziher, "Muhammedanisches Recht in Theorie und Wirklichkeit" *Zeitschrift jür vergleichende Rechtswissenschaft,* vol. 8 (1889), pp. 408–418.

63 J. Schacht and G.H. Bousquet, (eds.), *Selected Works of C. Snouck Hurgronje,*

(Leiden: e.j. Brill, 1957), p. 290.
64 A. Udovitch, *op. cit., passim.*
65 S.D. Goitein, "Commercial and Family Partnerships in the Countries of Medieval Islam", *Islamic Studies,* vol. 3 (1964), p. 318.
66 A. Udovitch, *op. cit.,* p. 258.
67 *Ibid.,* p. 261.
68 Haim Gerber, *op. cit., passim.*
69 Those who argue that *fiqh* was not related to the reality even in the medieval era should find this sentence, written in the seventeenth-century Bursa, interesting.
70 Haim Gerber, *op. cit.,* pp. 112, 113, 114.
71 Haim Gerber, *op. cit.,* p. 118.
72 Besides the Ottoman evidence presented above there is also the possibility that the *mudaraba* might have found application in Mughal India, where it was known as *"avog".* See; Irfan Habib, "Usury in Medieval India", *Comparative Studies in Society and History;* vol. 6, No. 4 (1964), p. 405.
73 Haim Gerber, "The Muslim Law of Partnerships in Ottoman Court Records," *Studia Islamica,* LIII, pp. 111.
74 Y. Firestone, "Production and Trade in an Islamic Context: *Sharika* contracts in the Transitional Economy of Northern Samaria: 1853–1943", *IJMES,* pp. 185–207.
75 The reader will note that this Palestinian *musaka* appears to have been quite different than the Turkish *musaka* observed by Gerber in Bursa. Since Firestone's information is limited to what is given between the brackets, Gerber's definition should be preferred.
76 Y. Firestone, *op. cit.,* p. 195.
77 *Ibid.,* p. 195.
78 *Ibid.,* p. 196.
79 Udovitch, *Partnership and Profit,* p. 188, 189.
80 Y. Firestone, *op. cit.,* p. 197.
81 Y. Firestone, *ibid.,* p. 203.
82 Firestone's interpretation, *ibid.,* p. 203; see *mejelle,* art. 1409, 1338, 1342.
83 Y. Firestone, *ibid.,* p. 204.
84 *Ibid.,* p. 206, 207.
85 *Newsweek,* 26th Sept., 1983, p. 53.